Selected Poems

BY TED HUGHES

The Hawk in the Rain
Lupercal
Wodwo
Crow: From the Life and Songs of the Crow
Cave Birds: An Alchemical Cave Drama
Gaudete
Remains of Elmet
Moortown
Selected Poems (*with Thom Gunn*)
Selected Poems 1957–1967

Seneca's Oedipus (*adapted by Ted Hughes*)

for children
Season Songs
Under the North Star
The Earth-Owl and Other Moon-People
The Iron Man: A Story in Five Nights
Meet My Folks!
Nessie the Mannerless Monster
How the Whale Became
The Coming of the Kings and other plays

edited by Ted Hughes
Poetry in the Making: An Anthology of Poems and
    Programmes from *Listening and Writing*
A Choice of Emily Dickinson's Verse
A Choice of Shakespeare's Verse

Selected Poems
1957–1981

TED HUGHES

faber and faber

This selection first published in 1982
by Faber and Faber Limited
3 Queen Square London WC1N 3AU
Filmset by King's English Typesetters Ltd Cambridge
Printed in Great Britain by
Richard Clay (The Chaucer Press) Ltd
Bungay Suffolk

© Ted Hughes, 1982

British Library Cataloguing in Publication Data

Hughes, Ted
Selected poems 1957–1981
I. Title
821'.914   PR6058.U37

ISBN 0–571–11877–1 ✓
ISBN 0–571–11916–6 Pbk

CONTENTS

The Thought-Fox

I imagine this midnight moment's forest:
Something else is alive
Beside the clock's loneliness
And this blank page where my fingers move.

Through the window I see no star:
Something more near
Though deeper within darkness
Is entering the loneliness:

Cold, delicately as the dark snow
A fox's nose touches twig, leaf;
Two eyes serve a movement, that now
And again now, and now, and now

Sets neat prints into the snow
Between trees, and warily a lame
Shadow lags by stump and in hollow
Of a body that is bold to come

Across clearings, an eye,
A widening deepening greenness,
Brilliantly, concentratedly,
Coming about its own business

Till, with a sudden sharp hot stink of fox
It enters the dark hole of the head.
The window is starless still; the clock ticks,
The page is printed.

Song

O lady, when the tipped cup of the moon blessed you
You became soft fire with a cloud's grace;
The difficult stars swam for eyes in your face;
You stood, and your shadow was my place:
You turned, your shadow turned to ice
    O my lady.

O lady, when the sea caressed you
You were a marble of foam, but dumb.
When will the stone open its tomb?
When will the waves give over their foam?
You will not die, nor come home,
    O my lady.

O lady, when the wind kissed you
You made him music for you were a shaped shell.
I follow the waters and the wind still
Since my heart heard it and all to pieces fell
Which your lovers stole, meaning ill,
    O my lady.

O lady, consider when I shall have lost you
The moon's full hands, scattering waste,
The sea's hands, dark from the world's breast,
The world's decay where the wind's hands have passed,
And my head, worn out with love, at rest
In my hands, and my hands full of dust,
    O my lady.

The Jaguar

The apes yawn and adore their fleas in the sun.
The parrots shriek as if they were on fire, or strut
Like cheap tarts to attract the stroller with the nut.
Fatigued with indolence, tiger and lion

Lie still as the sun. The boa-constrictor's coil
Is a fossil. Cage after cage seems empty, or
Stinks of sleepers from the breathing straw.
It might be painted on a nursery wall.

But who runs like the rest past these arrives
At a cage where the crowd stands, stares, mesmerized,
As a child at a dream, at a jaguar hurrying enraged
Through prison darkness after the drills of his eyes

On a short fierce fuse. Not in boredom—
The eye satisfied to be blind in fire,
By the bang of blood in the brain deaf the ear—
He spins from the bars, but there's no cage to him

More than to the visionary his cell:
His stride is wildernesses of freedom:
The world rolls under the long thrust of his heel.
Over the cage floor the horizons come.

Famous Poet

Stare at the monster: remark
How difficult it is to define just what
Amounts to monstrosity in that
Very ordinary appearance. Neither thin nor fat,
Hair between light and dark,

And the general air
Of an apprentice—say, an apprentice house-
Painter amid an assembly of famous
Architects: the demeanour is of mouse,
Yet is he monster.

First scrutinize those eyes
For the spark, the effulgence: nothing. Nothing there
But the haggard stony exhaustion of a near-
Finished variety artist. He slumps in his chair
Like a badly hurt man, half life-size.

Is it his dreg-boozed inner demon
Still tankarding from tissue and follicle
The vital fire, the spirit electrical
That puts the gloss on a normal hearty male?
Or is it women?

The truth—bring it on
With black drapery, drums and funeral tread
Like a great man's coffin—no, no, he is not dead
But in this truth surely half-buried:
Once, the humiliation

Of youth and obscurity,
The autoclave of heady ambition trapped,
The fermenting of the yeasty heart stopped—
Burst with such pyrotechnics the dull world gaped
   And "Repeat that!" still they cry.

   But all his efforts to concoct
The old heroic bang from their money and praise
From the parent's pointing finger and the child's amaze,
Even from the burning of his wreathed bays,
   Have left him wrecked: wrecked,

   And monstrous, so,
As a Stegosaurus, a lumbering obsolete
Arsenal of gigantic horn and plate
From a time when half the world still burned, set
   To blink behind bars at the zoo.

Soliloquy

Whenever I am got under my gravestone
Sending my flowers up to stare at the church-tower,
Gritting my teeth in the chill from the church-floor,
I shall praise God heartily, to see gone,

As I look round at old acquaintance there,
Complacency from the smirk of every man,
And every attitude showing its bone,
And every mouth confessing its crude shire;

But I shall thank God thrice heartily
To be lying beside women who grimace
Under the commitments of their flesh,
And not out of spite or vanity.

The Horses

I climbed through woods in the hour-before-dawn dark.
Evil air, a frost-making stillness,

Not a leaf, not a bird,—
A world cast in frost. I came out above the wood

Where my breath left tortuous statues in the iron light.
But the valleys were draining the darkness

Till the moorline—blackening dregs of the brightening grey—
Halved the sky ahead. And I saw the horses:

Huge in the dense grey—ten together—
Megalith-still. They breathed, making no move,

With draped manes and tilted hind-hooves,
Making no sound.

I passed: not one snorted or jerked its head.
Grey silent fragments

Of a grey silent world.

I listened in emptiness on the moor-ridge.
The curlew's tear turned its edge on the silence.

Slowly detail leafed from the darkness. Then the sun
Orange, red, red erupted.

Silently, and splitting to its core tore and flung cloud,
Shook the gulf open, showed blue,

And the big planets hanging—
I turned

Stumbling in the fever of a dream, down towards
The dark woods, from the kindling tops,

And came to the horses.
                    There, still they stood,
But now steaming and glistening under the flow of light,

Their draped stone manes, their tilted hind-hooves
Stirring under a thaw while all around them

The frost showed its fires. But still they made no sound.
Not one snorted or stamped,

Their hung heads patient as the horizons
High over valleys, in the red levelling rays—

In din of the crowded streets, going among the years, the faces,
May I still meet my memory in so lonely a place

Between the streams and the red clouds, hearing curlews,
Hearing the horizons endure.

Fallgrief's Girlfriends

Not that she had no equal, not that she was
His before flesh was his or the world was;
Not that she had the especial excellence
To make her cat-indolence and shrew-mouth
Index to its humanity. Her looks
Were what a good friend would not comment on.
If he made flattery too particular,
Admiring her cookery or lipstick,
Her eyes reflected painfully. Yet not that
He pitied her: he did not pity her.

"Any woman born", he said, "having
What any woman born cannot but have,
Has as much of the world as is worth more
Than wit or lucky looks can make worth more;
And I, having what I have as a man
Got without choice, and what I have chosen,
City and neighbour and work, am poor enough
To be more than bettered by a worst woman.
Whilst I am this muck of man in this
Muck of existence, I shall not seek more
Than a muck of a woman: wit and lucky looks
Were a ring disabling this pig-snout,
And a tin clasp on this diamond."

By this he meant to break out of the dream
Where's admiration's giddy mannequin
Leads every sense to motley; he meant to stand naked
Awake in the pitch dark where the animal runs,
Where the insects couple as they murder each other,
Where the fish outwait the water.

The chance changed him:
He has found a woman with such wit and looks
He can brag of her in every company.

Egg-Head

    A leaf's otherness,
The whaled monstered sea-bottom, eagled peaks
And stars that hang over hurtling endlessness,
    With manslaughtering shocks

    Are let in on his sense:
So many a one has dared to be struck dead
Peeping through his fingers at the world's ends,
    Or at an ant's head.

    But better defence
Than any militant pride are the freebooting crass
Veterans of survival and those champions
    Forgetfulness, madness.

    Brain in deft opacities,
Walled in translucencies, shuts out the world's knocking
With a welcome, and to wide-eyed deafnesses
    Of prudence lets it speak.

    Long the eggshell head's
Fragility rounds and resists receiving the flash
Of the sun, the bolt of the earth: and feeds
    On the yolk's dark and hush

    Of a helplessness coming
By feats of torpor, by circumventing sleights
Of stupefaction, juggleries of benumbing,
    By lucid sophistries of sight

    To a staturing "I am",
To the upthrust affirmative head of a man.
Braggart-browed complacency in most calm
    Collusion with his own

Dewdrop frailty
Must stop the looming mouth of the earth with a pin-
Point cipher, with a blank-stare courtesy
    Confront it and preen,

    Spurn it muck under
His foot-clutch, and, opposing his eye's flea-red
Fly-catching fervency to the whelm of the sun,
    Trumpet his own ear dead.

The Man Seeking Experience
Enquires His Way
of a Drop of Water

"This water droplet, charity of the air,
Out of the watched blue immensity—
(Where, where are the angels?) out of the draught in the door,
The Tuscarora, the cloud, the cup of tea,
The sweating victor and the decaying dead bird—
This droplet has travelled far and studied hard.

"Now clings on the cream paint of our kitchen wall.
Aged eye! This without heart-head-nerve lens
Which saw the first and earth-centering jewel
Spark upon darkness, behemoth bulk and lumber
Out of the instant flash, and man's hand
Hoist him upright, still hangs clear and round.

"Having studied a journey in the high
Cathedralled brain, the mole's ear, the fish's ice,
The abattoir of the tiger's artery,
The slum of the dog's bowel, and there is no place
His bright look has not bettered, and problem none
But he has brought it to solution.

"Venerable elder! Let us learn of you.
Read us a lesson, a plain lesson how
Experience has worn or made you anew,
That on this humble kitchen wall hang now,
O dew that condensed of the breath of the Word
On the mirror of the syllable of the Word."

So he spoke, aloud, grandly, then stood
For an answer, knowing his own nature all
Droplet-kin, sisters and brothers of lymph and blood,
Listened for himself to speak for the drop's self.
This droplet was clear simple water still.
It no more responded than the hour-old child

Does to finger-toy or coy baby-talk,
But who lies long, long and frowningly
Unconscious under the shock of its own quick
After that first alone-in-creation cry
When into the mesh of sense, out of the dark,
Blundered the world-shouldering monstrous "I".

Meeting

He smiles in a mirror, shrinking the whole
Sun-swung zodiac of light to a trinket shape
  On the rise of his eye: it is a role

In which he can fling a cape,
And outloom life like Faustus. But once when
  On an empty mountain slope

A black goat clattered and ran
Towards him, and set forefeet firm on a rock
  Above and looked down

A square-pupilled yellow-eyed look
The black devil head against the blue air,
  What gigantic fingers took

Him up and on a bare
Palm turned him close under an eye
  That was like a living hanging hemisphere

And watched his blood's gleam with a ray
Slow and cold and ferocious as a star
  Till the goat clattered away.

Wind

This house has been far out at sea all night,
The woods crashing through darkness, the booming hills,
Winds stampeding the fields under the window
Floundering black astride and blinding wet

Till day rose; then under an orange sky
The hills had new places, and wind wielded
Blade-light, luminous black and emerald,
Flexing like the lens of a mad eye.

At noon I scaled along the house-side as far as
The coal-house door. Once I looked up—
Through the brunt wind that dented the balls of my eyes
The tent of the hills drummed and strained its guyrope,

The fields quivering, the skyline a grimace,
At any second to bang and vanish with a flap:
The wind flung a magpie away and a black-
Back gull bent like an iron bar slowly. The house

Rang like some fine green goblet in the note
That any second would shatter it. Now deep
In chairs, in front of the great fire, we grip
Our hearts and cannot entertain book, thought,

Or each other. We watch the fire blazing,
And feel the roots of the house move, but sit on,
Seeing the window tremble to come in,
Hearing the stones cry out under the horizons.

October Dawn

October is marigold, and yet
A glass half full of wine left out

To the dark heaven all night, by dawn
Has dreamed a premonition

Of ice across its eye as if
The ice-age had begun its heave.

The lawn overtrodden and strewn
From the night before, and the whistling green

Shrubbery are doomed. Ice
Has got its spearhead into place.

First a skin, delicately here
Restraining a ripple from the air;

Soon plate and rivet on pond and brook;
Then tons of chain and massive lock

To hold rivers. Then, sound by sight
Will Mammoth and Sabre-tooth celebrate

Reunion while a fist of cold
Squeezes the fire at the core of the world,

Squeezes the fire at the core of the heart,
And now it is about to start.

Bayonet Charge

Suddenly he awoke and was running—raw
In raw-seamed hot khaki, his sweat heavy,
Stumbling across a field of clods towards a green hedge
That dazzled with rifle fire, hearing
Bullets smacking the belly out of the air—
He lugged a rifle numb as a smashed arm;
The patriotic tear that had brimmed in his eye
Sweating like molten iron from the center of his chest,—

In bewilderment then he almost stopped—
In what cold clockwork of the stars and the nations
Was he the hand pointing that second? He was running
Like a man who has jumped up in the dark and runs
Listening between his footfalls for the reason
Of his still running, and his foot hung like
Statuary in mid-stride. Then the shot-slashed furrows

Threw up a yellow hare that rolled like a flame
And crawled in a threshing circle, its mouth wide
Open silent, its eyes standing out.
He plunged past with his bayonet toward the green hedge,
King, honour, human dignity, etcetera
Dropped like luxuries in a yelling alarm
To get out of that blue crackling air
His terror's touchy dynamite.

Six Young Men

The celluloid of a photograph holds them well,—
Six young men, familiar to their friends.
Four decades that have faded and ochre-tinged
This photograph have not wrinkled the faces or the hands.
Though their cocked hats are not now fashionable,
Their shoes shine. One imparts an intimate smile,
One chews a grass, one lowers his eyes, bashful,
One is ridiculous with cocky pride—
Six months after this picture they were all dead.

All are trimmed for a Sunday jaunt. I know
That bilberried bank, that thick tree, that black wall,
Which are there yet and not changed. From where these sit
You hear the water of seven streams fall
To the roarer in the bottom, and through all
The leafy valley a rumouring of air go.
Pictured here, their expressions listen yet,
And still that valley has not changed its sound
Though their faces are four decades under the ground.

This one was shot in an attack and lay
Calling in the wire, then this one, his best friend,
Went out to bring him in and was shot too;
And this one, the very moment he was warned
From potting at tin-cans in no-man's land,
Fell back dead with his rifle-sights shot away.
The rest, nobody knows what they came to,
But come to the worst they must have done, and held it
Closer than their hope; all were killed.

Here see a man's photograph,
The locket of a smile, turned overnight
Into the hospital of his mangled last
Agony and hours; see bundled in it
His mightier-than-a-man dead bulk and weight:
And on this one place which keeps him alive
(In his Sunday best) see fall war's worst
Thinkable flash and rending, onto his smile
Forty years rotting into soil.

That man's not more alive whom you confront
And shake by the hand, see hale, hear speak loud,
Than any of these six celluloid smiles are,
Nor prehistoric or fabulous beast more dead;
No thought so vivid as their smoking-blood:
To regard this photograph might well dement,
Such contradictory permanent horrors here
Smile from the single exposure and shoulder out
One's own body from its instant and heat.

The Martyrdom of Bishop Farrar

Burned by Bloody Mary's men at Caermarthen. "If I flinch from the pain
of the burning, believe not the doctrine that I have preached." (His
words on being chained to the stake.)

Bloody Mary's venomous flames can curl:
They can shrivel sinew and char bone
Of foot, ankle, knee, and thigh, and boil
Bowels, and drop his heart a cinder down;
And her soldiers can cry, as they hurl
Logs in the red rush: "This is her sermon."

The sullen-jowled watching Welsh townspeople
Hear him crack in the fire's mouth; they see what
Black oozing twist of stuff bubbles the smell
That tars and retches their lungs: no pulpit
Of his ever held their eyes so still,
Never, as now his agony, his wit.

An ignorant means to establish ownership
Of his flock! Thus their shepherd she seized
And knotted him into this blazing shape
In their eyes, as if such could have cauterized
The trust they turned towards him, and branded on
Its stump her claim, to outlaw question.

So it might have been: seeing their exemplar
And teacher burned for his lessons to black bits,
Their silence might have disowned him to her,
And hung up what he had taught with their Welsh hats:
Who sees his blasphemous father struck by fire
From heaven, might well be heard to speak no oaths.

But the fire that struck here, come from Hell even,
Kindled little heavens in his words
As he fed his body to the flame alive.
Words which, before they will be dumbly spared,
Will burn their body and be tongued with fire
Make paltry folly of flesh and this world's air.

When they saw what annuities of hours
And comfortable blood he burned to get
His words a bare honouring in their ears,
The shrewd townsfolk pocketed them hot:
Stamp was not current but they rang and shone
As good gold as any queen's crown.

Gave all he had, and yet the bargain struck
To a merest farthing his whole agony,
His body's cold-kept miserdom of shrieks
He gave uncounted, while out of his eyes,
Out of his mouth, fire like a glory broke,
And smoke burned his sermon into the skies.

Mayday on Holderness

This evening, motherly summer moves in the pond.
I look down into the decomposition of leaves—
The furnace door whirling with larvae.

From Hull's sunset smudge
Humber is melting eastward, my south skyline:
A loaded single vein, it drains
The effort of the inert North—Sheffield's ores.
Bog pools, dregs of toadstools, tributary
Graves, dunghills, kitchens, hospitals.
The unkillable North Sea swallows it all.
Insects, drunken, drop out of the air.

                          Birth-soils,
The sea-salts, scoured me, cortex and intestine,
To receive these remains.
As the incinerator, as the sun,
As the spider, I had a whole world in my hands.
Flowerlike, I loved nothing.
Dead and unborn are in God comfortable.
What a length of gut is growing and breathing—
This mute eater, biting through the mind's
Nursery floor, with eel and hyena and vulture,
With creepy-crawly and the root,
With the sea-worm, entering its birthright.

The stars make pietas. The owl announces its sanity.

The crow sleeps glutted and the stoat begins.
There are eye-guarded eggs in these hedgerows,
Hot haynests under the roots in burrows.
Couples at their pursuits are laughing in the lanes.

The North Sea lies soundless. Beneath it
Smoulder the wars: to heart-beats, bomb, bayonet.
"Mother, Mother!" cries the pierced helmet.
Cordite oozings of Gallipoli,

Curded to beastings, broached my palate,
The expressionless gaze of the leopard,
The coils of the sleeping anaconda,
The nightlong frenzy of shrews.

Crow Hill

The farms are oozing craters in
Sheer sides under the sodden moors:
When it is not wind it is rain,
Neither of which will stop at doors:
One will damp beds and the other shake
Dreams beneath sleep it cannot break.

Between the weather and the rock
Farmers make a little heat;
Cows that sway a bony back,
Pigs upon delicate feet
Hold off the sky, trample the strength
That shall level these hills at length.

Buttoned from the blowing mist
Walk the ridges of ruined stone.
What humbles these hills has raised
The arrogance of blood and bone,
And thrown the hawk upon the wind,
And lit the fox in the dripping ground.

A Woman Unconscious

Russia and America circle each other;
Threats nudge an act that were without doubt
A melting of the mould in the mother,
Stones melting about the root,

The quick of the earth burned out:
The toil of all our ages a loss
With leaf and insect. Yet flitting thought
(Not to be thought ridiculous)

Shies from the world-cancelling black
Of its playing shadow: it has learned
That there's no trusting (trusting to luck)
Dates when the world's due to be burned;

That the future's no calamitous change
But a malingering of now,
Histories, towns, faces that no
Malice or accident much derange.

And though bomb be matched against bomb,
Though all mankind wince out and nothing endure—
Earth gone in an instant flare—
Did a lesser death come

Onto the white hospital bed
Where one, numb beyond her last of sense,
Closed her eyes on the world's evidence
And into pillows sunk her head.

Strawberry Hill

A stoat danced on the lawns here
To the music of the maskers;
Drinking the staring hare dry, bit
Through grammar and corset. They nailed to a door

The stoat with the sun in its belly,
But its red unmanageable life
Has licked the stylist out of their skulls
Has sucked that age like an egg and gone off

Along ditches where flies and leaves
Overpower our tongues, got into some grave—
Not a dog to follow it down—
Emerges, thirsting, in far Asia, in Brixton.

Fourth of July

The hot shallows and seas we bring our blood from
Slowly dwindled; cooled
To sewage estuary, to trout-stocked tarn.
Even the Amazon's taxed and patrolled

To set laws by the few jaws—
Piranha and jaguar.
Columbus' huckstering breath
Blew inland through North America

Killing the last of the mammoths.
The right maps have no monsters.
Now the mind's wandering elementals,
Ousted from their traveller-told

Unapproachable islands,
From their heavens and their burning underworld,
Wait dully at the traffic crossing,
Or lean over headlines, taking nothing in.

Esther's Tomcat

Daylong this tomcat lies stretched flat
As an old rough mat, no mouth and no eyes,
Continual wars and wives are what
Have tattered his ears and battered his head.

Like a bundle of old rope and iron
Sleeps till blue dusk. Then reappear
His eyes, green as ringstones: he yawns wide red,
Fangs fine as a lady's needle and bright.

A tomcat sprang at a mounted knight,
Locked round his neck like a trap of hooks
While the knight rode fighting its clawing and bite.
After hundreds of years the stain's there

On the stone where he fell, dead of the tom:
That was at Barnborough. The tomcat still
Grallochs odd dogs on the quiet,
Will take the head clean off your simple pullet,

Is unkillable. From the dog's fury,
From gunshot fired point-blank he brings
His skin whole, and whole
From owlish moons of bekittenings

Among ashcans. He leaps and lightly
Walks upon sleep, his mind on the moon.
Nightly over the round world of men,
Over the roofs go his eyes and outcry.

Wilfred Owen's Photographs

When Parnell's Irish in the House
Pressed that the British Navy's cat-
O-nine-tails be abolished, what
Shut against them? It was
Neither Irish nor English nor of that
Decade, but of the species.

Predictably, Parliament
Squared against the motion. As soon
Let the old school tie be rent
Off their necks, and give thanks, as see gone
No shame but a monument—
Trafalgar not better known.

"To discontinue it were as much
As ship not powder and cannonballs
But brandy and women" (Laughter). Hearing which
A witty profound Irishman calls
For a "cat" into the House, and sits to watch
The gentry fingering its stained tails.

Whereupon . . .
                quietly, unopposed,
The motion was passed.

Hawk Roosting

I sit in the top of the wood, my eyes closed.
Inaction, no falsifying dream
Between my hooked head and hooked feet:
Or in sleep rehearse perfect kills and eat.

The convenience of the high trees!
The air's buoyancy and the sun's ray
Are of advantage to me;
And the earth's face upward for my inspection.

My feet are locked upon the rough bark.
It took the whole of Creation
To produce my foot, my each feather:
Now I hold Creation in my foot

Or fly up, and revolve it all slowly—
I kill where I please because it is all mine.
There is no sophistry in my body:
My manners are tearing off heads—

The allotment of death.
For the one path of my flight is direct
Through the bones of the living.
No arguments assert my right:

The sun is behind me.
Nothing has changed since I began.
My eye has permitted no change.
I am going to keep things like this.

Fire-Eater

Those stars are the fleshed forebears
Of these dark hills, bowed like labourers,

And of my blood.

The death of a gnat is a star's mouth: its skin,
Like Mary's or Semele's, thin

As the skin of fire:
A star fell on her, a sun devoured her.

My appetite is good
Now to manage both Orion and Dog

With a mouthful of earth, my staple.
Worm-sort, root-sort, going where it is profitable.

A star pierces the slug,

The tree is caught up in the constellations.
My skull burrows among antennae and fronds.

The Bull Moses

A hoist up and I could lean over
The upper edge of the high half-door,
My left foot ledged on the hinge, and look in at the byre's
Blaze of darkness: a sudden shut-eyed look
Backward into the head.
                        Blackness is depth
Beyond star. But the warm weight of his breathing,
The ammoniac reek of his litter, the hotly-tongued,
Mash of his cud, steamed against me.
Then, slowly, as onto the mind's eye—
The brow like masonry, the deep-keeled neck:
Something come up there onto the brink of the gulf,
Hadn't heard of the world, too deep in itself to be called to,
Stood in sleep. He would swing his muzzle at a fly
But the square of sky where I hung, shouting, waving,
Was nothing to him; nothing of our light
Found any reflection in him.
                        Each dusk the farmer led him
Down to the pond to drink and smell the air,
And he took no pace but the farmer
Led him to take it, as if he knew nothing
Of the ages and continents of his fathers,
Shut, while he wombed, to a dark shed
And steps between his door and the duckpond;
The weight of the sun and the moon and the world hammered
To a ring of brass through his nostrils. He would raise
His streaming muzzle and look out over the meadows,
But the grasses whispered nothing awake, the fetch
Of the distance drew nothing to momentum
In the locked black of his powers. He came strolling gently back,
Paused neither toward the pig-pens on his right,
Nor toward the cow-byres on his left: something
Deliberate in his leisure, some beheld future

Founding in his quiet.
                    I kept the door wide,
Closed it after him and pushed the bolt.

Cat and Mouse

On the sheep-cropped summit, under hot sun,
The mouse crouched, staring out the chance
It dared not take,
    Time and a world
Too old to alter, the five mile prospect—
Woods, villages, farms—hummed its heat-heavy
Stupor of life.
    Whether to two
Feet or four, how are prayers contracted!
Whether in God's eye or the eye of a cat.

View of a Pig

The pig lay on a barrow dead.
It weighed, they said, as much as three men.
Its eyes closed, pink white eyelashes.
Its trotters stuck straight out.

Such weight and thick pink bulk
Set in death seemed not just dead.
It was less than lifeless, further off.
It was like a sack of wheat.

I thumped it without feeling remorse.
One feels guilty insulting the dead,
Walking on graves. But this pig
Did not seem able to accuse.

It was too dead. Just so much
A poundage of lard and pork.
Its last dignity had entirely gone.
It was not a figure of fun.

Too dead now to pity.
To remember its life, din, stronghold
Of earthly pleasure as it had been,
Seemed a false effort, and off the point.

Too deadly factual. Its weight
Oppressed me—how could it be moved?
And the trouble of cutting it up!
The gash in its throat was shocking, but not pathetic.

Once I ran at a fair in the noise
To catch a greased piglet
That was faster and nimbler than a cat,
Its squeal was the rending of metal.

Pigs must have hot blood, they feel like ovens.
Their bite is worse than a horse's—
They chop a half-moon clean out.
They eat cinders, dead cats.

Distinctions and admirations such
As this one was long finished with.
I stared at it a long time. They were going to scald it,
Scald it and scour it like a doorstep.

The Retired Colonel

Who lived at the top end of our street
Was a Mafeking stereotype, ageing.
Came, face pulped scarlet with kept rage,
For air past our gate.
Barked at his dog knout and whipcrack
And cowerings of India: five or six wars
Stiffened in his reddened neck;
Brow bull-down for the stroke.

Wife dead, daughters gone, lived on
Honouring his own caricature.
Shot through the heart with whisky wore
The lurch like ancient courage, would not go down
While posterity's trash stood, held
His habits like a last stand, even
As if he had Victoria rolled
In a Union Jack in that stronghold.

And what if his sort should vanish?
The rabble starlings roar upon
Trafalgar. The man-eating British lion
By a pimply age brought down.
Here's his head mounted, though only in rhymes,
Beside the head of the last English
Wolf (those starved gloomy times!)
And the last sturgeon of Thames.

November

The month of the drowned dog. After long rain the land
Was sodden as the bed of an ancient lake,
Treed with iron and birdless. In the sunk lane
The ditch—a seep silent all summer—

Made brown foam with a big voice: that, and my boots
On the lane's scrubbed stones, in the gulleyed leaves,
Against the hill's hanging silence;
Mist silvering the droplets on the bare thorns

Slower than the change of daylight.
In a let of the ditch a tramp was bundled asleep;
Face tucked down into beard, drawn in
Under his hair like a hedgehog's. I took him for dead,

But his stillness separated from the death
Of the rotting grass and the ground. A wind chilled,
And a fresh comfort tightened through him,
Each hand stuffed deeper into the other sleeve.

His ankles, bound with sacking and hairy hand,
Rubbed each other, resettling. The wind hardened;
A puff shook a glittering from the thorns,
And again the rains' dragging grey columns

Smudged the farms. In a moment
The fields were jumping and smoking; the thorns
Quivered, riddled with the glassy verticals.
I stayed on under the welding cold

Watching the tramp's face glisten and the drops on his coat
Flash and darken. I thought what strong trust
Slept in him—as the trickling furrows slept,
And the thorn-roots in their grip on darkness;

And the buried stones, taking the weight of winter;
The hill where the hare crouched with clenched teeth.
Rain plastered the land till it was shining
Like hammered lead, and I ran, and in the rushing wood

Shuttered by a black oak leaned.
The keeper's gibbet had owls and hawks
By the neck, weasels, a gang of cats, crows:
Some, stiff, weightless, twirled like dry bark bits

In the drilling rain. Some still had their shape,
Had their pride with it; hung, chins on chests,
Patient to outwait these worst days that beat
Their crowns bare and dripped from their feet.

Relic

I found this jawbone at the sea's edge:
There, crabs, dogfish, broken by the breakers or tossed
To flap for half an hour and turn to a crust
Continue the beginning. The deeps are cold:
In that darkness camaraderie does not hold;
Nothing touches but, clutching, devours. And the jaws,
Before they are satisfied or their stretched purpose
Slacken, go down jaws; go gnawn bare. Jaws
Eat and are finished and the jawbone comes to the beach:
This is the sea's achievement; with shells,
Vertebrae, claws, carapaces, skulls.

Time in the sea eats its tail, thrives, casts these
Indigestibles, the spars of purposes
That failed far from the surface. None grow rich
In the sea. This curved jawbone did not laugh
But gripped, gripped and is now a cenotaph.

An Otter

I

Underwater eyes, an eel's
Oil of water body, neither fish nor beast is the otter:
   Four-legged yet water-gifted, to outfish fish;
      With webbed feet and long ruddering tail
      And a round head like an old tomcat.

   Brings the legend of himself
From before wars or burials, in spite of hounds and vermin-poles;
   Does not take root like the badger. Wanders, cries;
      Gallops along land he no longer belongs to;
      Re-enters the water by melting.

   Of neither water nor land. Seeking
Some world lost when first he dived, that he cannot come at since,
   Takes his changed body into the holes of lakes;
      As if blind, cleaves the stream's push till he licks
      The pebbles of the source; from sea

   To sea crosses in three nights
Like a king in hiding. Crying to the old shape of the starlit land,
   Over sunken farms where the bats go round,
      Without answer. Till light and birdsong come
      Walloping up roads with the milk wagon.

II

The hunt's lost him. Pads on mud,
Among sedges, nostrils a surface bead,
The otter remains, hours. The air,
Circling the globe, tainted and necessary,

Mingling tobacco-smoke, hounds and parsley,
Comes carefully to the sunk lungs.
So the self under the eye lies,
Attendant and withdrawn. The otter belongs

In double robbery and concealment—
From water that nourishes and drowns, and from land
That gave him his length and the mouth of the hound.
He keeps fat in the limpid integument

Reflections live on. The heart beats thick,
Big trout muscle out of the dead cold;
Blood is the belly of logic; he will lick
The fishbone bare. And can take stolen hold

On a bitch otter in a field full
Of nervous horses, but linger nowhere.
Yanked above hounds, reverts to nothing at all,
To this long pelt over the back of a chair.

Witches

Once was every woman the witch
To ride a weed the ragwort road;
Devil to do whatever she would:
Each rosebud, every old bitch.

Did they bargain their bodies or no?
Proprietary the devil that
Went horsing on their every thought
When they scowled the strong and lucky low.

Dancing in Ireland nightly, gone
To Norway (the ploughboy bridled),
Nightlong under the blackamoor spraddled,
Back beside their spouse by dawn

As if they had dreamed all. Did they dream it?
Oh, our science says they did.
It was all wishfully dreamed in bed.
Small psychology would unseam it.

Bitches still sulk, rosebuds blow,
And we are devilled. And though these weep
Over our harms, who's to know
Where their feet dance while their heads sleep?

Thrushes

Terrifying are the attent sleek thrushes on the lawn,
More coiled steel than living—a poised
Dark deadly eye, those delicate legs
Triggered to stirrings beyond sense—with a start, a bounce, a stab
Overtake the instant and drag out some writhing thing.
No indolent procrastinations and no yawning stares.
No sighs or head-scratchings. Nothing but bounce and stab
And a ravening second.

Is it their single-minded-sized skulls, or a trained
Body, or genius, or a nestful of brats
Gives their days this bullet and automatic
Purpose? Mozart's brain had it, and the shark's mouth
That hungers down the blood-smell even to a leak of its own
Side and devouring of itself: efficiency which
Strikes too streamlined for any doubt to pluck at it
Or obstruction deflect.

With a man it is otherwise. Heroisms on horseback,
Outstripping his desk-diary at a broad desk,
Carving at a tiny ivory ornament
For years: his act worships itself—while for him,
Though he bends to be blent in the prayer, how loud and above
                                                    what
Furious spaces of fire do the distracting devils
Orgy and hosannah, under what wilderness
Of black silent waters weep.

Snowdrop

Now is the globe shrunk tight
Round the mouse's dulled wintering heart.
Weasel and crow, as if moulded in brass,
Move through an outer darkness
Not in their right minds,
With the other deaths. She, too, pursues her ends,
Brutal is the stars of this month,
Her pale head heavy as metal.

Pike

Pike, three inches long, perfect
Pike in all parts, green tigering the gold.
Killers from the egg: the malevolent aged grin.
They dance on the surface among the flies.

Or move, stunned by their own grandeur
Over a bed of emerald, silhouette
Of submarine delicacy and horror.
A hundred feet long in their world.

In ponds, under the heat-struck lily pads—
Gloom of their stillness:
Logged on last year's black leaves, watching upwards.
Or hung in an amber cavern of weeds

The jaws' hooked clamp and fangs
Not to be changed at this date;
A life subdued to its instrument;
The gills kneading quietly, and the pectorals.

Three we kept behind glass,
Jungled in weed: three inches, four,
And four and a half: fed fry to them—
Suddenly there were two. Finally one.

With a sag belly and the grin it was born with.
And indeed they spare nobody.
Two, six pounds each, over two feet long,
High and dry and dead in the willow-herb—

One jammed past its gills down the other's gullet:
The outside eye stared: as a vice locks—
The same iron in this eye
Though its film shrank in death.

A pond I fished, fifty yards across,
Whose lilies and muscular tench
Had outlasted every visible stone
Of the monastery that planted them—

Stilled legendary depth:
It was as deep as England. It held
Pike too immense to stir, so immense and old
That past nightfall I dared not cast

But silently cast and fished
With the hair frozen on my head
For what might move, for what eye might move.
The still splashes on the dark pond,

Owls hushing the floating woods
Frail on my ear against the dream
Darkness beneath night's darkness had freed,
That rose slowly towards me, watching.

Sunstroke

Frightening the blood in its tunnel
The mowing machine ate at the field of grass.

My eyes had been glared dark. Through a red heat
The cradled guns, damascus, blued, flared—

At every stir sliding their molten embers
Into my head. Sleekly the clover

Bowed and flowed backward
Over the saw-set swimming blades

Till the blades bit—roots, stones, ripped into red—
Some baby's body smoking among the stalks.

Reek of paraffin oil and creosote
Swabbing my lungs doctored me back

Laid on a sack in the great-beamed engine-shed.
I drank at stone, at iron of plough and harrow;

Dulled in a pit, heard thick walls of rain
And voices in swaddled confinement near me

Warm as veins. I lay healing
Under the ragged length of a dog fox

That dangled head downward from one of the beams,
With eyes open, forepaws strained at a leap—

Also surprised by the rain.

Cleopatra to the Asp

The bright mirror I braved: the devil in it
Loved me like my soul, my soul:
Now that I seek myself in a serpent
My smile is fatal.

Nile moves in me; my thighs splay
Into the squalled Mediterranean;
My brain hides in that Abyssinia
Lost armies foundered towards.

Desert and river unwrinkle again.
Seeming to bring them the waters that make drunk
Caesar, Pompey, Antony I drank.
Now let the snake reign.

A half-deity out of Capricorn,
This rigid Augustus mounts
With his sword virginal indeed; and has shorn
Summarily the moon-horned river

From my bed. May the moon
Ruin him with virginity! Drink me, now, whole
With coiled Egypt's past; then from my delta
Swim like a fish toward Rome.

Thistles

Against the rubber tongues of cows and the hoeing hands of men
Thistles spike the summer air
Or crackle open under a blue-black pressure.

Every one a revengeful burst
Of resurrection, a grasped fistful
Of splintered weapons and Icelandic frost thrust up

From the underground stain of a decayed Viking.
They are like pale hair and the gutturals of dialects.
Every one manages a plume of blood.

Then they grow grey, like men.
Mown down, it is a feud. Their sons appear,
Stiff with weapons, fighting back over the same ground.

Still Life

Outcrop stone is miserly

With the wind. Hoarding its nothings,
Letting wind run through its fingers,
It pretends to be dead of lack.
Even its grimace is empty,
Warted with quartz pebbles from the sea's womb.

It thinks it pays no rent,
Expansive in the sun's summerly reckoning.
Under rain, it gleams exultation blackly
As if receiving interest.
Similarly, it bears the snow well.

Wakeful and missing little and landmarking
The fly-like dance of the planets,
The landscape moving in sleep,
It expects to be in at the finish.
Being ignorant of this other, this harebell,

That trembles, as under threats of death,
In the summer turf's heat-rise,
And in which—filling veins
Any known name of blue would bruise
Out of existence—sleeps, recovering,

The maker of the sea.

Her Husband

Comes home dull with coal-dust deliberately
To grime the sink and foul towels and let her
Learn with scrubbing brush and scrubbing board
The stubborn character of money.

And let her learn through what kind of dust
He has earned his thirst and the right to quench it
And what sweat he has exchanged for his money
And the blood-weight of money. He'll humble her

With new light on her obligations.
The fried, woody chips, kept warm two hours in the oven,
Are only part of her answer.
Hearing the rest, he slams them to the fire back

And is away round the house-end singing
"Come back to Sorrento" in a voice
Of resounding corrugated iron.
Her back has bunched into a hump as an insult.

For they will have their rights.
Their jurors are to be assembled
From the little crumbs of soot. Their brief
Goes straight up to heaven and nothing more is heard of it.

Cadenza

The violinist's shadow vanishes.

The husk of a grasshopper
Sucks a remote cyclone and rises.

The full, bared throat of a woman walking water,
The loaded estuary of the dead.

And I am the cargo
Of a coffin attended by swallows.

And I am the water
Bearing the coffin that will not be silent.

The clouds are full of surgery and collision
But the coffin escapes—a black diamond,

A ruby brimming blood,
An emerald beating its shores,

The sea lifts swallow wings and flings
A summer lake open,

Sips and bewilders its reflection,
Till the whole sky dives shut like a burned land back to its spark—

A bat with a ghost in its mouth
Struck at by lightnings of silence—

Blue with sweat, the violinist
Crashes into the orchestra, which explodes.

Ghost Crabs

At nightfall, as the sea darkens,
A depth darkness thickens, mustering from the gulfs and the
                                        submarine badlands,
To the sea's edge. To begin with
It looks like rocks uncovering, mangling their pallor.
Gradually the labouring of the tide
Falls back from its productions,
Its power slips back from glistening nacelles, and they are crabs.
Giant crabs, under flat skulls, staring inland
Like a packed trench of helmets.
Ghosts, they are ghost-crabs.
They emerge
An invisible disgorging of the sea's cold
Over the man who strolls along the sands.
They spill inland, into the smoking purple
Of our woods and towns—a bristling surge
Of tall and staggering spectres
Gliding like shocks through water.
Our walls, our bodies, are no problem to them.
Their hungers are homing elsewhere.
We cannot see them or turn our minds from them.
Their bubbling mouths, their eyes
In a slow mineral fury
Press through our nothingness where we sprawl on beds,
Or sit in rooms. Our dreams are ruffled maybe,
Or we jerk awake to the world of possessions
With a gasp, in a sweat burst, brains jamming blind
Into the bulb-light. Sometimes, for minutes, a sliding
Staring
Thickness of silence
Presses between us. These crabs own this world.
All night, around us or through us,
They stalk each other, they fasten on to each other,

They mount each other, they tear each other to pieces,
They utterly exhaust each other.
They are the powers of this world.
We are their bacteria,
Dying their lives and living their deaths.
At dawn, they sidle back under the sea's edge.
They are the turmoil of history, the convulsion
In the roots of blood, in the cycles of concurrence.
To them, our cluttered countries are empty battleground.
All day they recuperate under the sea.
Their singing is like a thin sea-wind flexing in the rocks of
                                                    a headland,
Where only crabs listen.

They are God's only toys.

Boom

And faces at the glutted shop-windows
Gaze into the bottomless well
Of wishes

Like rearlights away up the long road
Toward an earth-melting dawn
Of the same thing, but staler.

More More More
Meaning Air Water Life
Cry the mouths

That are filling with burning ashes.

II   BAR-ROOM TV

On a flaked ridge of the desert

Outriders have found foul water. They say nothing;
With the cactus and the petrified tree
Crouch numbed by a wind howling all
Visible horizons equally empty.

The wind brings dust and nothing
Of the wives, the children, the grandmothers
With the ancestral bones, who months ago
Left the last river,

Coming at the pace of oxen.

III   TUTORIAL

Like a propped skull,
His humour is mediaeval.

What are all those tomes? Tomb-boards
Pressing the drying remains of men.
He brings some out, we stew them up to a dark amber and sit
                                                    sipping.

He is fat, this burst bearskin, but his mind is an electric mantis
Plucking the heads and legs off words, the homunculi.
I am thin but I can hardly move my bulk, I go round and
                    round numbly under the ice of the North Pole.

This scholar dribbling tea
Onto his tie, straining pipe-gargle
Through the wharf-weed that ennobles

The mask of enquiry, advancing into the depths like a harbour,
Like a sphynx cliff,
Like the papery skull of a fish

Lodged in dune sand, with a few straws,
Rifled by dry cold.
His words

Twitch and rustle, twitch
And rustle.
The scarred world looks through their gaps.

I listen
With bleak eyeholes.

IV WINO

Grape is my mulatto mother
In this frozen whited country. Her veined interior
Hangs hot open for me to re-enter
The blood-coloured glasshouse against which the stone world
Thins to a dew and steams off—
Diluting neither my blood cupful
Nor its black undercurrent. I swell in there, soaking.
Till the grape for sheer surfeit of me
Vomits me up. I'm found
Feeble as a babe, but renewed.

V KAFKA

And he is an owl
He is an owl, "Man" tattooed in his armpit
Under the broken wing
(Stunned by the wall of glare, he fell here)
Under the broken wing of huge shadow that twitches across the
floor.

He is a man in hopeless feathers.

Second Glance at a Jaguar

Skinful of bowls he bowls them,
The hip going in and out of joint, dropping the spine
With the urgency of his hurry
Like a cat going along under thrown stones, under cover,
Glancing sideways, running
Under his spine. A terrible, stump-legged waddle
Like a thick Aztec disemboweller,
Club-swinging, trying to grind some square
Socket between his hind legs round,
Carrying his head like a brazier of spilling embers,
And the black bit of his mouth, he takes it
Between his back teeth, he has to wear his skin out,
He swipes a lap at the water-trough as he turns,
Swivelling the ball of his heel on the polished spot,
Showing his belly like a butterfly.
At every stride he has to turn a corner
In himself and correct it. His head
Is like the worn down stump of another whole jaguar,
His body is just the engine shoving it forward,
Lifting the air up and shoving on under,
The weight of his fangs hanging the mouth open,
Bottom jaw combing the ground. A gorged look,
Gangster, club-tail lumped along behind gracelessly,
He's wearing himself to heavy ovals,
Muttering some mantrah, some drum-song of murder
To keep his rage brightening, making his skin
Intolerable, spurred by the rosettes, the Cain-brands,
Wearing the spots off from the inside,
Rounding some revenge. Going like a prayer-wheel,
The head dragging forward, the body keeping up,
The hind legs lagging. He coils, he flourishes
The blackjack tail as if looking for a target,
Hurrying through the underworld, soundless.

Fern

Here is the fern's frond, unfurling a gesture,
Like a conductor whose music will now be pause
And the one note of silence
To which the whole earth dances gravely.

The mouse's ear unfurls its trust,
The spider takes up her bequest,
And the retina
Reins the creation with a bridle of water.

And, among them, the fern
Dances gravely, like the plume
Of a warrior returning, under the low hills,

Into his own kingdom.

A Wind Flashes the Grass

Leaves pour blackly across.
We cling to the earth, with glistening eyes, pierced afresh by the
tree's cry.

And the incomprehensible cry
From the boughs, in the wind
Sets us listening for below words,
Meanings that will not part from the rock.

The trees thunder in unison, on a gloomy afternoon
And the ploughman grows anxious, his tractor becomes terrible,
His memory litters downwind
And the shadow of his bones tosses darkly on the air.

The trees suddenly storm to a stop, in a hush
Against the sky, where the field ends.
They crowd there shuddering
And wary, like horses bewildered by lightning.

The stirring of their twigs against the dark, travelling sky
Is the oracle of the earth.

They too are afraid they too are momentary
Streams rivers of shadow

Bowled Over

By kiss of death, bullet on brow,
No more life can overpower
That first infatuation, world cannot
Ever be harder or clearer or come
Closer than when it arrived there

Spinning its patched fields, churches
Trees where nightingales sang in broad daylight
And the vast flaring blue skirts of seas—
Then sudden insubordination
Of boredom and sleep

When the eyes could not find their keys
Or the neck remember what mother whispered
Or the body stand to its word.

Desertion in the face of a bullet!

Buried without honours.

Root, Stem, Leaf

I

A match spluttering near out, before it touches the moors,
You start, threatened by your own tears.
But not your skin, not doors, not borders
Will be proof against your foraging
Through everything unhuman or human
To savour and own the dimensions of woman
As water does those of water.
                              But the river
Is a prayer to its own waters
Where the circulation of our world is pouring
In stillness—
Everyone's peace, no less your own peace.

Out of bedrock your blood's operation
Carves your eyes clear not so quickly
As your mouth dips deeper
Into the massed darkness.

II

Having taken her slowly by surprise
For eighty years
The hills have won, their ring is closed.

The field-walls float their pattern
Over her eye
Whether she looks outward or inward.

Nothing added, nothing taken away.
Year after year the trout in the pools
Grow heavy and vanish, without ever emerging.

Foxglove, harebell neither protest nor hope
On the steep slope where she climbs.
Out of nothing she grew here simply

Also suffering to be merely flowerlike

But with the stone agony growing in her joints
And eyes, dimming with losses, widening for losses.

III

To be a girl's diary,

Crumbling, glanced into
By strange smiles, in a saleroom,
Where the dust is of eyes and hearts, in proportion,
As well as of old shoes, meteors, and dung . . .

To be an heirloom spoon, blackening
Among roots in a thorn-hedge, forgetful
Of flavours as of tongues,
Fleeting towards heavenly dispersal,
Walked by spiders . . .

Nightfall collects the stars
Only in a manner of speaking.

Everything is inheriting everything.

Stations

Suddenly his poor body
Had its drowsy mind no longer
For insulation.

Before the funeral service foundered
The lifeboat coffin had shaken to pieces
And the great stars were swimming through where he had been.

For a while

The stalk of the tulip at the door that had outlived him,
And his jacket, and his wife, and his last pillow
Clung to each other.

II

I can understand the haggard eyes
Of the old

Dry wrecks

Broken by seas of which they could drink nothing.

III

They have sunk into deeper service. They have gone down
To labour with God on the beaches. They fatten
Under the haddock's thumb. They rejoice
Through the warped mouth of the flounder

And are nowhere they are not here I know nothing
Cries the poulterer's hare hanging
Upside down above the pavement
Staring into a bloody bag Not here

Cry the eyes from the depths

Of the mirror's seamless sand.

IV

You are a wild look—out of an egg
Laid by your absence.

In the great Emptiness you sit complacent,
Blackbird in wet snow.

If you could make only one comparison—
Your condition is miserable, you would give up.

But you, from the start, surrender to total Emptiness,
Then leave everything to it.

Absence. It is your own
Absence

Weeps its respite through your accomplished music,
Wraps its cloak dark about your feeding.

V

Whether you say it, think it, know it
Or not, it happens, it happens as
Over rails over
The neck the wheels leave
The head with its vocabulary useless,
Among the flogged plantains.

The Green Wolf

My neighbour moves less and less, attempts less.
If his right hand still moves, it is a farewell
Already days posthumous.

But the left hand seems to freeze,
And the left leg with its crude plumbing,
And the left half jaw and the left eyelid and the words all the huge
cries

Frozen in his brain his tongue cannot unfreeze—
While somewhere through a dark heaven
The dark bloodclot moves in.

I watch it approaching but I cannot fear it.
The punctual evening star,
Worse, the warm hawthorn blossoms, their foam,

Their palls of deathly perfume,
Worst of all the beanflower
Badged with jet like the ear of the tiger

Unmake and remake me. That star
And that flower and that flower
And living mouth and living mouth all

One smouldering annihilation
Of old brains, old bowels, old bodies
In the scarves of dew, the wet hair of nightfall.

Scapegoats and Rabies

Soldiers are marching singing down the lane

They get their abandon
From the fixed eyes of girls, from their own
Armed anonymity
And from having finally paid up
All life might demand. They get
Their heroic loom
From the statue stare of old women,
From the trembling chins of old men,
From the napes and bow legs of toddlers,
From the absolute steel
Of their automatic rifles, and the lizard spread
Of their own fingers, and from their bird stride.
They get their facelessness
From the blank, deep meadows and the muddling streams
And the hill's eyeless outlook,
The babel of gravestones, the mouldering
Of letters and citations
On rubbish dumps. They get the drumming engine
Of their boots
From their hearts,
From their eyeless, earless hearts,
Their brainless hearts. And their bravery
From the dead millions of ghosts
Marching in their boots, cumbering their bodies,
Staring from under their brows, concentrating
Toward a repeat performance. And their hopelessness
From the millions of the future
Marching in their boots, blindfold and riddled,

Rotten heads on their singing shoulders,
The blown-off right hand swinging to the stride
Of the stump-scorched and blown-off legs
Helpless in the terrible engine of the boots.

The soldiers go singing down the deep lane
Wraiths into the bombardment of afternoon sunlight,
Whelmed under the flashing onslaught of the barley,
Strangled in the drift of honeysuckle.

Their bodiless voices rally on the slope and again
In the far woods

Then settle like dust
Under the ancient burden of the hill.

II   THE MASCOT

Somewhere behind the lines, over the map,
The General's face hangs in the dark, like a lantern.

Every shell that bursts
Blows it momentarily out, and he has to light it.

Every bullet that bangs off
Goes in at one of his ears and out at the other.

Every attack every rout
Storms through that face, like a flood through a footbridge.

Every new-dead ghost
Comes to that worn-out blood for its death-ration.

Every remotest curse, weighted with a bloodclot,
Enters that ear like a blowfly.

Knives, forks, spoons divide his brains.
The supporting earth, and the night around him,

Smoulder like the slow, curing fire
Of a Javanese head-shrinker.

Nothing remains of the *tête d'armée* but the skin—
A dangling parchment lantern

Slowly revolving to right, revolving to left,

Trembling a little with the incessant pounding,

Over the map, empty in the ring of light.

III   WIT'S END

The General commits his emptiness to God.

And in place of his eyes
Crystal balls
Roll with visions.

And his voice rises
From the dead fragments of men

A Frankenstein
A tank
A ghost
Roaming the impossible
Raising the hair on men's heads.

84

His hand
Has swept the battlefield flat as a sheet of foolscap.
He writes:

I AM A LANTERN
              IN THE HAND
                          OF A BLIND PEOPLE

IV   TWO MINUTES' SILENCE

The soldier's boots, beautifully bulled,
Are graves
On the assembly line
Rolls Royces
Opera boxes
Double beds
Cafes
With big smiles and laced-up eyes

His stockings
Are his own intestines
Cut into lengths—
They wear better and are
Nobody else's loss,
So he needn't charge diffidently

His battledress
Is Swanwhite's undies
Punch and Judy curtains
The Queen's pajamas
The Conjuror's hankie

The flapping sheet
Of the shithouse phantom

85

His helmet
Is a Ministry pisspot

His rifle
Is a Thames turd

And away downwind he runs, over no-man's-land,
In a shouting flight
From his own stink

Into the mushroom forest

Watched from the crowded walls.

V   THE RED CARPET

So the leaves trembled.

He leaned for a moment
Into the head-on leaden blast of ghost
From death's doorway
Then fell forward, under his equipment.
But though the jungle morass has gripped him to the knees
His outflung left hand clawed and got a hold
On Notting Hill
His brow banged hard down once then settled gently
Onto Hampstead Heath
The thumb of his twisted, smashed right hand
Settled in numb snugness
Across the great doorway of St Paul's
His lips oozed soft words and blood bubbles
Into the Chalk Farm railway cutting
Westminster knuckled his riddled chest
His belt-buckle broke Clapham
His knees his knees were dissolving in the ebb of the Channel

nd there he lay alive
is body full of lights, the restaurants seethed,
e groaned in the pushing of traffic that would not end
he girls strolled and their perfumes gargled in his throat
nd in the holes in his chest
nd though he could not lift his eyes to the streetlights
nd though he could not stir either hand
e knew in that last stride, that last
en thousand league effort, and even off balance,
e had made it home. And he called—

to mud.

gain the leaves trembled.

linters flew off Big Ben.

Stealing Trout on a May Morning

I park the car half in the ditch and switch off and sit.
The hot astonishment of my engine's arrival
Sinks through 5 a.m. silence and frost.
At the end of a long gash
An atrocity through the lace of first light
I sit with the reeking instrument.
I am on delicate business.
I want the steel to be cold instantly
And myself secreted three fields away
And the farms, back under their blankets, supposing a plane

passed

Because this is no wilderness you can just rip into.
Every leaf is plump and well-married,
Every grain of soil of known lineage, well-connected.
And the gardens are like brides fallen asleep
Before their weddings have properly begun.
The orchards are the hushed maids, fresh from convent . . . .
It is too hushed, something improper is going to happen.
It is too ghostly proper, all sorts of liveried listenings
Tiptoe along the lanes and peer over hedges.

I listen for the eyes jerked open on pillows,
Their dreams washed with sudden ugly petroleum.
They need only look out at a sheep.
Every sheep within two miles
Is nailing me accurately down
With its hellishly-shaven starved-priest expression.

I emerge. The air, after all, has forgotten everything.
The sugared spindles and wings of grass
Are etched on great goblets. A pigeon falls into space.
The earth is coming quietly and darkly up from a great depth,

Still under the surface. I am unknown,
But nothing is surprised. The tarmac of the road
Is velvet with sleep, the hills are out cold.
A new earth still in its wrappers
Of gauze and cellophane,
The frost from the storage still on its edges,
My privilege to poke and sniff.
The sheep are not much more than the primroses.
And the river there, amazed with itself,
Flexing and trying its lights
And unused fish, that are rising
And sinking for the sheer novelty
As the sun melts the hill's spine and the spilled light
Flows through their gills . . .

My mind sinks, rising and sinking.
And the opening arms of the sky forget me
Into the buried tunnel of hazels. There
My boot dangles down, till a thing black and sudden
Savages it, and the river is heaping under,
Alive and malevolent,
A coiling glider of shock, the space-black
Draining off the night-moor, under the hazels . . . .
But I drop and stand square in it, against it,
Then it is river again, washing its soul,
Its stones, its weeds, its fish, its gravels
And the rooty mouths of the hazels clear
Of the discolourings bled in
Off ploughlands and lanes . . . .

At first, I can hardly look at it—
The riding tables, the corrugated
Shanty roofs tightening
To braids, boilings where boulders throw up
Gestures of explosion, black splitting everywhere

To drowning skirts of whiteness, a slither of mirrors
Under the wading hazels. Here it is shallow,
Ropes my knees, lobbing fake boomerangs,
A drowned woman loving each ankle,
But I'm heavier and I wade with them upstream,
Flashing my blue minnow
Up the open throats of water
And across through the side of the rush
Of alligator escaping along there
Under the beards of the hazels, and I slice
The wild nape-hair off the bald bulges,
Till the tightrope of my first footholds
Tangles away downstream
And my bootsoles move as to magnets.

Soon I deepen. And now I meet the piling mob
Of voices and hurriers coming towards me
And tumbling past me. I press through a panic . . . .
This headlong river is a rout
Of tumbrils and gun-carriages, rags and metal,
All the funeral woe-drag of some overnight disaster
Mixed with planets, electrical storms and darkness
On a mapless moorland of granite,
Trailing past me with all its frights, its eyes
With what they have seen and still see,
They drag the flag off my head, a dark insistence
Tearing the spirits from my mind's edge and from under . . . .

To yank me clear takes the sudden, strong spine
Of one of the river's real members—
Thoroughly made of dew, lightning and granite
Very slowly over four years. A trout, a foot long,
Lifting its head in a shawl of water,
Fins banked stiff like a trireme
It forces the final curve wide, getting

A long look at me. So much for the horror
It has changed places.
                        Now I am a man in a painting
(Under the mangy, stuffed head of a fox)
Painted about 1905
Where the river steams and the frost relaxes
On the pear-blossoms. The brassy wood-pigeons
Bubble their colourful voices, and the sun
Rises upon a world well-tried and old.

Theology

No, the serpent did not
Seduce Eve to the apple.
All that's simply
Corruption of the facts.

Adam ate the apple.
Eve ate Adam.
The serpent ate Eve.
This is the dark intestine.

The serpent, meanwhile,
Sleeps his meal off in Paradise—
Smiling to hear
God's querulous calling.

Gog

I woke to a shout: 'I am Alpha and Omega.'
Rocks and a few trees trembled
Deep in their own country.
I ran and an absence bounded beside me.

The dog's god is a scrap dropped from the table.
The mouse's saviour is a ripe wheat grain.
Hearing the Messiah cry
My mouth widens in adoration.

How fat are the lichens!
They cushion themselves on the silence.
The air wants for nothing.
The dust, too, is replete.

What was my error? My skull has sealed it out.
My great bones are massed in me.
They pound on the earth, my song excites them.
I do not look at the rocks and trees, I am frightened of what they

see.

I listen to the song jarring my mouth
Where the skull-rooted teeth are in possession.
I am massive on earth. My feetbones beat on the earth
Over the sounds of motherly weeping . . .

Afterwards I drink at a pool quietly.
The horizon bears the rocks and trees away into twilight.
I lie down. I become darkness.

Darkness that all night sings and circles stamping.

Kreutzer Sonata

Now you have stabbed her good
A flower of unknown colour appallingly
Blackened by your surplus of bile
Blooms wetly on her dress.

"Your mystery! Your mystery! . . ."
All facts, with all absence of facts,
Exhale as the wound there
Drinks its roots and breathes them to nothing.

Vile copulation! Vile!——etcetera.
But now your dagger has outdone everybody's.
Say goodbye, for your wife's sweet flesh goes off,
Booty of the envious spirit's assault.

A sacrifice, not a murder.
One hundred and forty pounds
Of excellent devil, for God.
She tormented Ah demented you

With that fat lizard Trukachevsky,
That fiddling, leering penis.
Yet why should you castrate yourself
To be rid of them both?

Now you have stabbed her good
Trukachevsky is cut off
From any further operation on you,
And she can find nobody else.

Rest in peace, Tolstoy!
It must have taken supernatural greed
To need to corner all the meat in the world,
Even from your own hunger.

Out

I   THE DREAM TIME

My father sat in his chair recovering
From the four-year mastication by gunfire and mud,
Body buffeted wordless, estranged by long soaking
In the colours of mutilation.
                   His outer perforations
Were valiantly healed, but he and the hearth-fire, its blood-flicker
On biscuit-bowl and piano and table leg,
Moved into strong and stronger possession
Of minute after minute, as the clock's tiny cog
Laboured and on the thread of his listening
Dragged him bodily from under
The mortised four-year strata of dead Englishmen
He belonged with. He felt his limbs clearing
With every slight, gingerish movement. While I, small and four,
Lay on the carpet as his luckless double,
His memory's buried, immovable anchor,
Among jawbones and blown-off boots, tree-stumps, shellcases and
                                     craters,
Under rain that goes on drumming its rods and thickening
Its kingdom, which the sun has abandoned, and where nobody
Can ever again move from shelter.

II

The dead man in his cave beginning to sweat;
The melting bronze visor of flesh
Of the mother in the baby-furnace—
Nobody believes, it
Could be nothing, all

Undergo smiling at
The lulling of blood in
Their ears, their ears, their ears, their eyes
Are only drops of water and even the dead man suddenly
Sits up and sneezes—Atishoo!
Then the nurse wraps him up, smiling,
And, though faintly, the mother is smiling,
And it's just another baby.

As after being blasted to bits
The reassembled infantryman
Tentatively totters out, gazing around with the eyes
Of an exhausted clerk.

III   REMEMBRANCE DAY

The poppy is a wound, the poppy is the mouth
Of the grave, maybe of the womb searching—

A canvas-beauty puppet on a wire
Today whoring everywhere. It is years since I wore one.

It is more years
The shrapnel that shattered my father's paybook

Gripped me, and all his dead
Gripped him to a time

He no more than they could outgrow, but, cast into one, like iron,
Hung deeper than refreshing of ploughs

In the woe-dark under my mother's eye—
One anchor

Holding my juvenile neck bowed to the dunkings of the Atlantic.

So goodbye to that bloody-minded flower.

You dead bury your dead.
Goodbye to the cenotaphs on my mother's breasts.

Goodbye to all the remaindered charms of my father's survival

Let England close. Let the green sea-anemone close.

New Moon in January

A splinter, flicked
Into the wide eyeball,
Severs its warning.

The head, severed while staring,
Felt nothing, only
Tilted slightly.

O lone
Eyelash on the darkening
Stripe of blood, O sail of death!

Frozen
In ether
Unearthly

Shelley's faint-shriek
Trying to thaw while zero
Itself loses consciousness.

The Warriors of the North

Bringing their frozen swords, their salt-bleached eyes, their salt-
                                        bleached hair,
The snow's stupefied anvils in rows,
Bringing their envy,
The slow ships feelered Southward, snails over the steep sheen of
                                        the water-globe.

Thawed at the red and black disgorging of abbeys,
The bountiful, cleft casks,
The fluttered bowels of the women of dead burghers,
And the elaborate, patient gold of the Gaels.

To no end
But this timely expenditure of themselves,
A cash-down, beforehand revenge, with extra,
For the gruelling relapse and prolongueur of their blood

Into the iron arteries of Calvin.

The Rat's Dance

The rat is in the trap, it is in the trap,
And attacking heaven and earth with a mouthful of screeches like
                                                    torn tin,

An effective gag.
When it stops screeching, it pants

And cannot think
"This has no face, it must be God" or

"No answer is also an answer."
Iron jaws, strong as the whole earth

Are stealing its backbone
For a crumpling of the Universe with screechings,

For supplanting every human brain inside its skull with a rat-body
                                                    that knots and unknots,
A rat that goes on screeching,

Trying to uproot itself into each escaping screech,
But its long fangs bar that exit—

The incisors bared to the night spaces, threatening the
                                                    constellations,
The glitterers in the black, to keep off,

Keep their distance,
While it works this out.

The rat understands suddenly. It bows and is still,
With a little beseeching of blood on its nose-end.

Heptonstall

Black village of gravestones.
Skull of an idiot
Whose dreams die back
Where they were born.

Skull of a sheep
Whose meat melts
Under its own rafters.
Only the flies leave it.

Skull of a bird,
The great geographies
Drained to sutures
Of cracked windowsills.

Life tries.

Death tries.

The stone tries.

Only the rain never tires.

Skylarks

I

The lark begins to go up
Like a warning
As if the globe were uneasy—

Barrel-chested for heights,
Like an Indian of the high Andes,

A whippet head, barbed like a hunting arrow,

But leaden
With muscle
For the struggle
Against
Earth's centre.

And leaden
For ballast
In the rocketing storms of the breath.

Leaden
Like a bullet
To supplant
Life from its centre.

II

Crueller than owl or eagle

A towered bird, shot through the crested head
With the command, Not die

102

But climb

Climb

Sing

Obedient as to death a dead thing.

III

I suppose you just gape and let your gaspings
Rip in and out through your voicebox
                              O lark

And sing inwards as well as outwards
Like a breaker of ocean milling the shingle
                              O lark

O song, incomprehensibly both ways—
Joy! Help! Joy! Help!
                   O lark

IV

You stop to rest, far up, you teeter
Over the drop

But not stopping singing

Resting only for a second

Dropping just a little

Then up and up and up

Like a mouse with drowning fur
Bobbing and bobbing at the well-wall

Lamenting, mounting a little—

But the sun will not take notice
And the earth's centre smiles.

v

My idleness curdles
Seeing the lark labour near its cloud
Scrambling
In a nightmare difficulty
Up through the nothing

Its feathers thrash, its heart must be drumming like a motor,
As if it were too late, too late

Dithering in ether
Its song whirls faster and faster
And the sun whirls
The lark is evaporating
Till my eye's gossamer snaps
                        and my hearing floats back widely to earth

After which the sky lies blank open
Without wings, and the earth is a folded clod.

Only the sun goes silently and endlessly on with the lark's song.

VI

All the dreary Sunday morning
Heaven is a madhouse
With the voices and frenzies of the larks,

Squealing and gibbering and cursing

Heads flung back, as I see them,
Wings almost torn off backwards—far up

Like sacrifices set floating
The cruel earth's offerings

The mad earth's missionaries.

VII

Like those flailing flames
The lift from the fling of a bonfire
Claws dangling full of what they feed on

The larks carry their tongues to the last atom
Battering and battering their last sparks out at the limit—
So it's a relief, a cool breeze
When they've had enough, when they're burned out
And the sun's sucked them empty
And the earth gives them the O.K.

And they relax, drifting with changed notes

Dip and float, not quite sure if they may
Then they are sure and they stoop

And maybe the whole agony was for this

The plummeting dead drop

With long cutting screams buckling like razors

But just before they plunge into the earth

They flare and glide off low over grass, then up
To land on a wall-top, crest up,

Weightless,
Paid-up,
Alert,

Conscience perfect.

VIII

Manacled with blood,
Cuchulain listened bowed,
Strapped to his pillar (not to die prone)
Hearing the far crow
Guiding the near lark nearer
With its blind song

"That some sorry little wight more feeble and misguided than thyself
Take thy head
Thine ear
And thy life's career from thee."

Mountains

I am a fly if these are not stones,
If these are not stones, they are a finger—

Finger, shoulder, eye.
The air comes and goes over them as if attentively.

They were there yesterday and the world before yesterday,
Content with the inheritance,

Having no need to labour, only to possess the days,
Only to possess their power and their presence,

Smiling on the distance, their faces lit with the peace
Of the father's will and testament,

Wearing flowers in their hair, decorating their limbs
With the agony of love and the agony of fear and the agony of
death.

Pibroch

The sea cries with its meaningless voice
Treating alike its dead and its living,
Probably bored with the appearance of heaven
After so many millions of nights without sleep,
Without purpose, without self-deception.

Stone likewise. A pebble is imprisoned
Like nothing in the Universe.
Created for black sleep. Or growing
Conscious of the sun's red spot occasionally,
Then dreaming it is the foetus of God.

Over the stone rushes the wind
Able to mingle with nothing,
Like the hearing of the blind stone itself.
Or turns, as if the stone's mind came feeling
A fantasy of directions.

Drinking the sea and eating the rock
A tree struggles to make leaves—
An old woman fallen from space
Unprepared for these conditions.
She hangs on, because her mind's gone completely.

Minute after minute, aeon after aeon,
Nothing lets up or develops.
And this is neither a bad variant nor a tryout.
This is where the staring angels go through.
This is where all the stars bow down.

The Howling of Wolves

Is without world.

What are they dragging up and out on their long leashes of sound
That dissolve in the mid-air silence?

Then crying of a baby, in this forest of starving silences,
Brings the wolves running.
Tuning of a viola, in this forest delicate as an owl's ear,
Brings the wolves running—brings the steel traps clashing and
slavering,
The steel furred to keep it from cracking in the cold,
The eyes that never learn how it has come about
That they must live like this,

That they must live

Innocence crept into minerals.

The wind sweeps through and the hunched wolf shivers.
It howls you cannot say whether out of agony or joy.

The earth is under its tongue,
A dead weight of darkness, trying to see through its eyes.
The wolf is living for the earth.
But the wolf is small, it comprehends little.

It goes to and fro, trailing its haunches and whimpering horribly.

It must feed its fur.

The night snows stars and the earth creaks.

Gnat-Psalm

When the gnats dance at evening
Scribbling on the air, sparring sparely,
Scrambling their crazy lexicon,
Shuffling their dumb Cabala,
Under leaf shadow

Leaves only leaves
Between them and the broad swipes of the sun
Leaves muffling the dusty stabs of the late sun
From their frail eyes and crepuscular temperaments

Dancing
Dancing
Writing on the air, rubbing out everything they write
Jerking their letters into knots, into tangles
Everybody everybody else's yoyo

Immense magnets fighting around a centre

Not writing and not fighting but singing
That the cycles of this Universe are no matter
That they are not afraid of the sun
That the one sun is too near
It blasts their song, which is of all the suns
That they are their own sun
Their own brimming over
At large in the nothing
Their wings blurring the blaze
Singing

That they are the nails
In the dancing hands and feet of the gnat-god
That they hear the wind suffering
Through the grass
And the evening tree suffering

The wind bowing with long cat-gut cries
And the long roads of dust
Dancing in the wind
The wind's dance, the death-dance, entering the mountain
And the cow dung villages huddling to dust

But not the gnats, their agility
Has outleaped that threshold
And hangs them a little above the claws of the grass
Dancing
Dancing
In the glove shadows of the sycamore

A dance never to be altered
A dance giving their bodies to be burned

And their mummy faces will never be used

Their little bearded faces
Weaving and bobbing on the nothing
Shaken in the air, shaken, shaken
And their feet dangling like the feet of victims

O little Hasids
Ridden to death by your own bodies
Riding your bodies to death
You are the angels of the only heaven!

And God is an Almighty Gnat!
You are the greatest of all the galaxies!
My hands fly in the air, they are follies
My tongue hangs up in the leaves
My thoughts have crept into crannies

Your dancing

Your dancing

Rolls my staring skull slowly away into outer space.

Full Moon and Little Frieda

A cool small evening shrunk to a dog bark and the clank of a
bucket—

And you listening.
A spider's web, tense for the dew's touch.
A pail lifted, still and brimming—mirror
To tempt a first star to a tremor.

Cows are going home in the lane there, looping the hedges with
their warm wreaths of breath—
A dark river of blood, many boulders,
Balancing unspilled milk.

"Moon!" you cry suddenly, "Moon! Moon!"

The moon has stepped back like an artist gazing amazed at a work

That points at him amazed.

Wodwo

What am I? Nosing here, turning leaves over
Following a faint stain on the air to the river's edge
I enter water. What am I to split
The glassy grain of water looking upward I see the bed
Of the river above me upside down very clear
What am I doing here in mid-air? Why do I find
this frog so interesting as I inspect its most secret
interior and make it my own? Do these weeds
know me and name me to each other have they
seen me before, do I fit in their world? I seem
separate from the ground and not rooted but dropped
out of nothing casually I've no threads
fastening me to anything I can go anywhere
I seem to have been given the freedom
of this place what am I then? And picking
bits of bark off this rotten stump gives me
no pleasure and it's no use so why do I do it
me and doing that have coincided very queerly
But what shall I be called am I the first
have I an owner what shape am I what
shape am I am I huge if I go
to the end on this way past these trees and past these trees
till I get tired that's touching one wall of me
for the moment if I sit still how everything
stops to watch me I suppose I am the exact centre
but there's all this what is it roots
roots roots roots and here's the water
again very queer but I'll go on looking

Examination at the Womb-Door

Who owns these scrawny little feet?   *Death.*
Who owns this bristly scorched-looking face?   *Death.*
Who owns these still-working lungs?   *Death.*
Who owns this utility coat of muscles?   *Death.*
Who owns these unspeakable guts?   *Death.*
Who owns these questionable brains?   *Death.*
All this messy blood?   *Death.*
These minimum-efficiency eyes?   *Death.*
This wicked little tongue?   *Death.*
This occasional wakefulness?   *Death.*

Given, stolen, or held pending trial?
Held.

Who owns the whole rainy, stony earth?   *Death.*
Who owns all of space?   *Death.*

Who is stronger than hope?   *Death.*
Who is stronger than the will?   *Death.*
Stronger than love?   *Death.*
Stronger than life?   *Death.*

But who is stronger than death?

                    Me, evidently.

Pass, Crow.

A Childish Prank

Man's and woman's bodies lay without souls,
Dully gaping, foolishly staring, inert
On the flowers of Eden.
God pondered.

The problem was so great, it dragged him asleep.

Crow laughed.
He bit the Worm, God's only son,
Into two writhing halves.

He stuffed into man the tail half
With the wounded end hanging out.

He stuffed the head half headfirst into woman
And it crept in deeper and up
To peer out through her eyes
Calling its tail-half to join up quickly, quickly
Because O it was painful.

Man awoke being dragged across the grass.
Woman awoke to see him coming.
Neither knew what had happened.

God went on sleeping.

Crow went on laughing.

Crow's First Lesson

God tried to teach Crow how to talk.
"Love," said God. "Say, Love."
Crow gaped, and the white shark crashed into the sea
And went rolling downwards, discovering its own depth.

"No, no," said God, "Say Love. Now try it." LOVE."
Crow gaped, and a bluefly, a tsetse, a mosquito
Zoomed out and down
To their sundry flesh-pots.

"A final try," said God. "Now, LOVE."
Crow convulsed, gaped, retched and
Man's bodiless prodigious head
Bulbed out onto the earth, with swivelling eyes,
Jabbering protest—

And Crow retched again, before God could stop him.
And woman's vulva dropped over man's neck and tightened.
The two struggled together on the grass.
God struggled to part them, cursed, wept—

Crow flew guiltily off.

That Moment

When the pistol muzzle oozing blue vapour
Was lifted away
Like a cigarette lifted from an ashtray

And the only face left in the world
Lay broken
Between hands that relaxed, being too late

And the trees closed forever
And the streets closed forever

And the body lay on the gravel
Of the abandoned world
Among abandoned utilities
Exposed to infinity forever

Crow had to start searching for something to eat.

The Black Beast

Where is the Black Beast?
Crow, like an owl, swivelled his head.
Where is the Black Beast?
Crow hid in its bed, to ambush it.
Where is the Black Beast?
Crow sat in its chair, telling loud lies against the Black Beast.
Where is it?
Crow shouted after midnight, pounding the wall with a last.
Where is the Black Beast?
Crow split his enemy's skull to the pineal gland.
Where is the Black Beast?
Crow crucified a frog under a microscope, he peered into the brain
of a dogfish.

Where is the Black Beast?
Crow roasted the earth to a clinker, he charged into space—
Where is the Black Beast?
The silences of space decamped, space flitted in every direction—

Where is the Black Beast?
Crow flailed immensely through the vacuum, he screeched after
the disappearing stars—
Where is it? Where is the Black Beast?

Crow and the Birds

When the eagle soared clear through a dawn distilling of emerald.
When the curlew trawled in seadusk through a chime of
wineglasses
When the swallow swooped through a woman's song in a cavern
And the swift flicked through the breath of a violet

When the owl sailed clear of tomorrow's conscience
And the sparrow preened himself of yesterday's promise
And the heron laboured clear of the Bessemer upglare
And the bluetit zipped clear of lace panties
And the woodpecker drummed clear of the rotovator and the rose-
farm
And the peewit tumbled clear of the laundromat

While the bullfinch plumped in the apple bud
And the goldfinch bulbed in the sun
And the wryneck crooked in the moon
And the dipper peered from the dewball

Crow spraddled head-down in the beach-garbage, guzzling a
dropped ice-cream.

A Horrible Religious Error

When the serpent emerged, earth-bowel brown,
From the hatched atom
With its alibi self twisted around it

Lifting a long neck
And balancing that deaf and mineral stare
The sphynx of the final fact

And flexing on that double flameflicker tongue
A syllable like the rustling of the spheres

God's grimace writhed, a leaf in the furnace

And man's and woman's knees melted, they collapsed
Their neck-muscles melted, their brows bumped the ground
Their tears evacuated visibly
They whispered "Your will is our peace."

But Crow only peered.
                    Then took a step or two forward,
Grabbed this creature by the slackskin nape,

Beat the hell out of it, and ate it.

Owl's Song

He sang
How the swan blanched forever
How the wolf threw away its telltale heart
And the stars dropped their pretence
The air gave up appearances
Water went deliberately numb
The rock surrendered its last hope
And cold died beyond knowledge

He sang
How everything had nothing more to lose

Then sat still with fear

Seeing the clawtrack of star
Hearing the wingbeat of rock

And his own singing

The Contender

There was this man and he was the strongest
Of the strong.
He gritted his teeth like a cliff.
Though his body was sweeling away like a torrent on a cliff
Smoking towards dark gorges
There he nailed himself with nails of nothing

All the women in the world could not move him
They came their mouths deformed against stone
They came and their tears salted his nail-holes
Only adding their embitterment
To his effort
He abandoned his grin to them his grimace
In his face upwards body he lay face downwards
As a dead man adamant

His sandals could not move him they burst their thongs
And rotted from his fixture
All the men in the world could not move him
They wore at him with their shadows and little sounds
Their arguments were a relief
Like heather flowers
His belt could not endure the siege—it burst
And lay broken
He grinned
Little children came in chorus to move him
But he glanced at them out of his eye-corners
Over the edge of his grin
And they lost their courage for life

Oak forests came and went with the hawk's wing
Mountains rose and fell
He lay crucified with all his strength
On the earth
Grinning towards the sun
Through the tiny holes of his eyes
And towards the moon
And towards the whole paraphernalia of the heavens
Through the seams of his face
With the strings of his lips
Grinning through his atoms and decay
Grinning into the black
Into the ringing nothing
Through the bones of his teeth

Sometimes with eyes closed

In his senseless trial of strength.

Dawn's Rose

Is melting an old frost moon.

Agony under agony, the quiet of dust,
And a crow talking to stony skylines.

Desolate is the crow's puckered cry
As an old woman's mouth
When the eyelids have finished
And the hills continue.

A cry
Wordless
As the newborn baby's grieving
On the steely scales.

As the dull gunshot and its after-râle
Among conifers, in rainy twilight.

Or the suddenly dropped, heavily dropped
Star of blood on the fat leaf.

Apple Tragedy

So on the seventh day
The serpent rested.
God came up to him.
"I've invented a new game," he said.

The serpent stared in surprise
At this interloper.
But God said: "You see this apple?
I squeeze it and look—Cider."

The serpent had a good drink
And curled up into a questionmark.
Adam drank and said: "Be my god."
Eve drank and opened her legs

And called to the cockeyed serpent
And gave him a wild time.
God ran and told Adam
Who in drunken rage tried to hang himself in the orchard.

The serpent tried to explain, crying "Stop"
But drink was splitting his syllable
And Eve started screeching: "Rape! Rape!"
And stamping on his head.

Now whenever the snake appears she screeches
"Here it comes again! Help! O help!"
Then Adam smashes a chair on its head,
And God says: "I am well pleased"

And everything goes to hell.

Crow's Last Stand

Burning
        burning
                burning
                        there was finally something
The sun could not burn, that it had rendered
Everything down to—a final obstacle
Against which it raged and charred

And rages and chars

Limpid among the glaring furnace clinkers
The pulsing blue tongues and the red and the yellow
The green lickings of the conflagration

Limpid and black—

Crow's eye-pupil, in the tower of its scorched fort.

Lovesong

He loved her and she loved him
His kisses sucked out her whole past and future or tried to
He had no other appetite
She bit him she gnawed him she sucked
She wanted him complete inside her
Safe and sure forever and ever
Their little cries fluttered into the curtains

Her eyes wanted nothing to get away
Her looks nailed down his hands his wrists his elbows
He gripped her hard so that life
Should not drag her from that moment
He wanted all future to cease
He wanted to topple with his arms round her
Off that moment's brink and into nothing
Or everlasting or whatever there was
Her embrace was an immense press
To print him into her bones
His smiles were the garrets of a fairy palace
Where the real world would never come
Her smiles were spider bites
So he would lie still till she felt hungry
His words were occupying armies
Her laughs were an assassin's attempts
His looks were bullets daggers of revenge
Her glances were ghosts in the corner with horrible secrets
His whispers were whips and jackboots
Her kisses were lawyers steadily writing
His caresses were the last hooks of a castaway
Her love-tricks were the grinding of locks
And their deep cries crawled over the floors
Like an animal dragging a great trap

His promises were the surgeon's gag
Her promises took the top off his skull
She would get a brooch made of it
His vows pulled out all her sinews
He showed her how to make a love-knot
Her vows put his eyes in formalin
At the back of her secret drawer
Their screams stuck in the wall

Their heads fell apart into sleep like the two halves
Of a lopped melon, but love is hard to stop

In their entwined sleep they exchanged arms and legs
In their dreams their brains took each other hostage

In the morning they wore each other's face

Notes for a Little Play

First—the sun coming closer, growing by the minute.
Next—clothes torn off.
Without a goodbye
Faces and eyes evaporate.
Brains evaporate.
Hands arms legs feet head and neck
Chest and belly vanish
With all the rubbish of the earth.

And the flame fills all space.
The demolition is total
Except for two strange items remaining in the flames—
Two survivors, moving in the flames blindly.

Mutations—at home in the nuclear glare.

Horrors—hairy and slobbery, glossy and raw.

They sniff towards each other in the emptiness.

They fasten together. They seem to be eating each other.

But they are not eating each other.

They do not know what else to do.

They have begun to dance a strange dance.

And this is the marriage of these simple creatures—
Celebrated here, in the darkness of the sun,

Without guest or God.

The Lovepet

Was it an animal was it a bird?
She stroked it. He spoke to it softly.
She made her voice its happy forest.
He brought it out with sugarlump smiles.
Soon it was licking their kisses.

She gave it the strings of her voice which it swallowed
He gave it the blood of his face it grew eager
She gave it the liquorice of her mouth it began to thrive
He opened the aniseed of his future
And it bit and gulped, grew vicious, snatched
The focus of his eyes
She gave it the steadiness of her hand
He gave it the strength of his spine it ate everything

It began to cry what could they give it
They gave it their calendars it bolted their diaries
They gave it their sleep it gobbled their dreams
Even while they slept
It ate their bodyskin and the muscle beneath
They gave it vows its teeth clashed its starvation
Through every word they uttered

It found snakes under the floor it ate them
It found a spider horror
In their palms and ate it

They gave it double smiles and blank silence
It chewed holes in their carpets
They gave it logic
It ate the colour of their hair
They gave it every argument that would come
They gave it shouting and yelling they meant it

It ate the faces of their children
They gave it their photograph albums they gave it their records
It ate the colour of the sun
They gave it a thousand letters they gave it money
It ate their future complete it waited for them
Staring and starving
They gave it screams it had gone too far
It ate into their brains
It ate the roof
It ate lonely stone it ate wind crying famine
It went furiously off

They wept they called it back it could have everything
It stripped out their nerves chewed chewed flavourless
It bit at their numb bodies they did not resist
It bit into their blank brains they hardly knew

It moved bellowing
Through a ruin of starlight and crockery

It drew slowly off they could not move

It went far away they could not speak

How Water Began to Play

Water wanted to live
It went to the sun it came weeping back
Water wanted to live
It went to the trees they burned it came weeping back
They rotted it came weeping back
Water wanted to live
It went to the flowers they crumpled it came weeping back
It wanted to live
It went to the womb it met blood
It came weeping back
It went to the womb it met knife
It came weeping back
It went to the womb it met maggot and rottenness
It came weeping back it wanted to die

It went to time it went through the stone door
It came weeping back
It went searching through all space for nothingness
It came weeping back it wanted to die

Till it had no weeping left

It lay at the bottom of all things

Utterly worn out   utterly clear

Littleblood

O littleblood, hiding from the mountains in the mountains
Wounded by stars and leaking shadow
Eating the medical earth.

O littleblood, little boneless little skinless
Ploughing with a linnet's carcase
Reaping the wind and threshing the stones.

O littleblood, drumming in a cow's skull
Dancing with a gnat's feet
With an elephant's nose with a crocodile's tail.

Grown so wise grown so terrible
Sucking death's mouldy tits.

Sit on my finger, sing in my ear, O littleblood.

You Hated Spain

                    Spain frightened you. Spain
Where I felt at home. The blood-raw light,
The oiled anchovy faces, the African
Black edges to everything, frightened you.
Your schooling had somehow neglected Spain.
The wrought-iron grille, death and the Arab drum.
You did not know the language, your soul was empty
Of the signs, and the welding light
Made your blood shrivel. Bosch
Held out a spidery hand and you took it
Timidly, a bobby-sox American.
You saw right down to the Goya funeral grin
And recognised it, and recoiled
As your poems winced into chill, as your panic
Clutched back towards college America.
So we sat as tourists at the bullfight
Watching bewildered bulls awkwardly butchered,
Seeing the grey-faced matador, at the barrier
Just below us, straightening his bent sword
And vomiting with fear. And the horn
That hid itself inside the blowfly belly
Of the toppled picador punctured
What was waiting for you. Spain
Was the land of your dreams: the dust-red cadaver
You dared not wake with, the puckering amputations
No literature course had glamorized.
The juju land behind your African lips.
Spain was what you tried to wake up from
And could not. I see you, in moonlight,
Walking the empty wharf at Alicante
Like a soul waiting for the ferry,

A new soul, still not understanding,
Thinking it is still your honeymoon
In the happy world, with your whole life waiting,
Happy, and all your poems still to be found.

The Executioner

Fills up
Sun, moon, stars, he fills them up

With his hemlock—
They darken

He fills up the evening and the morning, they darken
He fills up the sea

He comes in under the blind filled-up heaven
Across the lightless filled-up face of water

He fills up the rivers he fills up the roads, like tentacles
He fills up the streams and the paths, like veins

The tap drips darkness darkness
Sticks to the soles of your feet

He fills up the mirror, he fills up the cup
He fills up your thoughts to the brims of your eyes

You just see he is filling the eyes of your friends
And now lifting your hand you touch at your eyes

Which he has completely filled up
You touch him

You have no idea what has happened
To what is no longer yours

It feels like the world
Before your eyes ever opened

The Knight

Has conquered. He has surrendered everything.

Now he kneels. He is offering up his victory
And unlacing his steel.

In front of him are the common wild stones of the earth—

The first and last altar
Onto which he lowers his spoils.

And that is right. He has conquered in earth's name.
Committing these trophies

To the small madness of roots, to the mineral stasis
And to rain.

An unearthly cry goes up.
The Universes squabble over him—

Here a bone, there a rag.
His sacrifice is perfect. He reserves nothing.

Skylines tug him apart, winds drink him,
Earth itself unravels him from beneath—

His submission is flawless.

Blueflies lift off his beauty.
Beetles and ants officiate

Pestering him with instructions.
His patience grows only more vast.

His eyes darken bolder in their vigil
As the chapel crumbles.

His spine survives its religion,
The texts moulder—

The quaint courtly language
Of wingbones and talons.

And already
Nothing remains of the warrior but his weapons

And his gaze.
Blades, shafts, unstrung bows—and the skull's beauty

Wrapped in the rags of his banner.
He is himself his banner and its rags.

While hour by hour the sun
Strengthens its revelation.

Bride and Groom Lie Hidden for Three Days

She gives him his eyes, she found them
Among some rubble, among some beetles

He gives her her skin
He just seemed to pull it down out of the air and lay it over her
She weeps with fearfulness and astonishment

She has found his hands for him, and fitted them freshly at the
                                                                    wrists
They are amazed at themselves, they go feeling all over her

He has assembled her spine, he cleaned each piece carefully
And sets them in perfect order
A superhuman puzzle but he is inspired
She leans back twisting this way and that,
                                using it and laughing, incredulous

Now she has brought his feet, she is connecting them
So that his whole body lights up

And he has fashioned her new hips
With all fittings complete and with newly wound coils, all
                                                            shiningly oiled
He is polishing every part, he himself can hardly believe it

They keep taking each other to the sun, they find they can easily
To test each new thing at each new step

And now she smooths over him the plates of his skull
So that the joints are invisible
And now he connects her throat,
                                her breasts and the pit of her stomach
With a single wire

She gives him his teeth, tying their roots
                                    to the centrepin of his body

He sets the little circlets on her fingertips

She stitches his body here and there with steely purple silk

He oils the delicate cogs of her mouth

She inlays with deep-cut scrolls the nape of his neck

He sinks into place the inside of her thighs

So, gasping with joy, with cries of wonderment
Like two gods of mud
Sprawling in the dirt, but with infinite care

They bring each other to perfection.

The Risen

He stands, filling the doorway
In the shell of earth.

He lifts wings, he leaves the remains of something,
A mess of offal, muddled as an afterbirth.

His each wingbeat—a convict's release.
What he carries will be plenty.

He slips behind the world's brow
As music escapes its skull, its clock and its skyline.

Under his sudden shadow, flames cry out among thickets.
When he soars, his shape

Is a cross, eaten by light,
On the Creator's face.

He shifts world weirdly as sunspots
Emerge as earthquakes.

A burning unconsumed,
A whirling tree—

Where he alights
A skin sloughs from a leafless apocalypse.

On his lens
Each atom engraves with a diamond.

In the wind-fondled crucible of his splendour
The dirt becomes God.

But when will he land
On a man's wrist.

A March Calf

Right from the start he is dressed in his best——his blacks and his
                                                                whites
Little Fauntleroy——quiffed and glossy,
A Sunday suit, a wedding natty get-up,
Standing in dunged straw

Under cobwebby beams, near the mud wall,
Half of him legs,
Shining-eyed, required nothing more
But that mother's milk come back often.

Everything else is in order, just as it is.
Let the summer skies hold off, for the moment.
This is just as he wants it.
A little at a time, of each new thing, is best.

Too much and too sudden is too frightening——
When I block the light, a bulk from space,
To let him in to his mother for a suck,
He bolts a yard or two, then freezes,

Staring from every hair in all directions,
Ready for the worst, shut up in his hopeful religion,
A little syllogism
With a wet blue-reddish muzzle, for God's thumb.

You see all his hopes bustling
As he reaches between the worn rails towards
The topheavy oven of his mother.
He trembles to grow, stretching his curl-tip tongue——

What did cattle ever find here
To make this dear little fellow
So eager to prepare himself?
He is already in the race, and quivering to win—

His new purpled eyeball swivel-jerks
In the elbowing push of his plans.
Hungry people are getting hungrier,
Butchers developing expertise and markets,

But he just wobbles his tail—and glistens
Within his dapper profile
Unaware of how his whole lineage
Has been tied up.

He shivers for feel of the world licking his side.
He is like an ember—one glow
Of lighting himself up
With the fuel of himself, breathing and brightening.

Soon he'll plunge out, to scatter his seething joy,
To be present at the grass,
To be free on the surface of such a wideness,
To find himself himself. To stand. To moo.

Apple Dumps

After the fiesta, the beauty-contests, the drunken wrestling
Of the blossom
Come some small ugly swellings, the dwarfish truths
Of the prizes.

After blushing and confetti, the breeze-blown bridesmaids, the
                                    shadowed snapshots
Of the trees in bloom
Come the gruelling knuckles, and the cracked housemaid's hands,
The workworn morning plainness of apples.

Unearthly was the hope, the wet star melting the gland,
Staggering the offer—
But pawky the real returns, not easy to see,
Dull and leaf-green, hidden, still-bitter, and hard.

The orchard flared wings, a new heaven, a dawn-lipped
                                    apocalypse
Kissing the sleeper—
The apples emerge, in the sun's black shade, among stricken trees,
A straggle of survivors, nearly all ailing.

Swifts

Fifteenth of May. Cherry blossom. The swifts
Materialize at the tip of a long scream
Of needle. "Look! They're back! Look!" And they're gone
On a steep

Controlled scream of skid
Round the house-end and away under the cherries. Gone.
Suddenly flickering in sky summit, three or four together,
Gnat-whisp frail, and hover-searching, and listening

For air-chills—are they too early? With a bowing
Power-thrust to left, then to right, then a flicker they
Tilt into a slide, a tremble for balance,
Then a lashing down disappearance

Behind elms.
                            They've made it again,
Which means the globe's still working, the Creation's
Still waking refreshed, our summer's
Still all to come—
                            And here they are, here they are again
Erupting across yard stones
Shrapnel-scatter terror. Frog-gapers,
Speedway goggles, international mobsters—

A bolas of three or four wire screams
Jockeying across each other
On their switchback wheel of death.
They swat past, hard-fletched,

Veer on the hard air, toss up over the roof,
And are gone again. Their mole-dark labouring,
Their lunatic limber scramming frenzy
And their whirling blades

Sparkle out into blue—
                    Not ours any more.
Rats ransacked their nests so now they shun us.
Round luckier houses now
They crowd their evening dirt-track meetings,

Racing their discords, screaming as if speed-burned,
Head-height, clipping the doorway
With their leaden velocity and their butterfly lightness,
Their too much power, their arrow-thwack into the eaves.

Every year a first-fling, nearly-flying
Misfit flopped in our yard,
Groggily somersaulting to get airborne.
He bat-crawled on his tiny useless feet, tangling his flails

Like a broken toy, and shrieking thinly
Till I tossed him up—then suddenly he flowed away under
His bowed shoulders of enormous swimming power,
Slid away along levels wobbling

On the fine wire they have reduced life to,
And crashed among the raspberries.
Then followed fiery hospital hours
In a kitchen. The moustached goblin savage

Nested in a scarf. The bright blank
Blind, like an angel, to my meat-crumbs and flies.
Then eyelids resting. Wasted clingers curled.
The inevitable balsa death.
                    Finally burial
For the husk
Of my little Apollo—

The charred scream
Folded in its huge power.

The Harvest Moon

The flame-red moon, the harvest moon,
Rolls along the hills, gently bouncing,
A vast balloon,
Till it takes off, and sinks upward
To lie in the bottom of the sky, like a gold doubloon.

The harvest moon has come,
Booming softly through heaven, like a bassoon.
And earth replies all night, like a deep drum.

So people can't sleep,
So they go out where elms and oak trees keep
A kneeling vigil, in a religious hush.
The harvest moon has come!

And all the moonlit cows and all the sheep
Stare up at her petrified, while she swells
Filling heaven, as if red hot, and sailing
Closer and closer like the end of the world.

Till the gold fields of stiff wheat
Cry "We are ripe, reap us!" and the rivers
Sweat from the melting hills.

A Cranefly in September

She is struggling through grass-mesh—not flying,
Her wide-winged, stiff, weightless basket-work of limbs
Rocking, like an antique wain, a top-heavy ceremonial cart
Across mountain summits
(Not planing over water, dipping her tail)
But blundering with long strides, long reachings, reelings
And ginger-glistening wings
From collision to collision.
Aimless in no particular direction,
Just exerting her last to escape out of the overwhelming
Of whatever it is, legs, grass,
The garden, the county, the country, the world—

Sometimes she rests long minutes in the grass forest
Like a fairytale hero, only a marvel can help her.
She cannot fathom the mystery of this forest
In which, for instance, this giant watches—
The giant who knows she cannot be helped in any way.

Her jointed bamboo fuselage,
Her lobster shoulders, and her face
Like a pinhead dragon, with its tender moustache,
And the simple colourless church windows of her wings
Will come to an end, in mid-search, quite soon.
Everything about her, every perfected vestment
Is already superfluous.
The monstrous excess of her legs and curly feet
Are a problem beyond her.
The calculus of glucose and chitin inadequate
To plot her through the infinities of the stems.

The frayed apple leaves, the grunting raven, the defunct tractor
Sunk in nettles, wait with their multiplications
Like other galaxies.
The sky's Northward September procession, the vast soft

armistice,

Like an Empire on the move,
Abandons her, tinily embattled
With her cumbering limbs and cumbered brain.

Goose

The White Bear, with smoking mouth, embraces
All the North.
The Wild Goose listens

South, south—
                    the Goose stretches his neck
Over the glacier.

And high, high
Turns the globe in his hands.

Hunts with his pack from star to star.
Sees the sun far down behind the world.

Sinks through fingers of light, with apricot breast,
To startle sleeping farms, at apple dawn,
With iceberg breath.

Then to and fro all Christmas, evening and morning,
Urging his linked team,
Clears the fowler's gun and the surf angler.

Homesick
Smells the first flower of the Northern Lights—

Clears the Lamb's cry, wrestles heaven,
Sets the globe turning.

Clears the dawns—a compass tolling
North, north.
                    North, north.

Wingbeat wading the flame of evening.

Till he dips his eyes
In the whale's music

Among the boom
Of calving glaciers

And wooing of wolves
And rumpus of walrus.

agle

wings dawns dark.
e Sun is hunting.
under collects, under granite eyebrows.

e horizons are ravenous.
e dark mountain has an electric eye.
e sun lowers its meat-hook.

s spread fingers measure a heaven, then a heaven.
s ancestors worship only him,
d his children's children cry to him alone.

s trapeze is a continent.
e Sun is looking for fuel
ith the gaze of a guillotine.

d already the White Hare crouches at the sacrifice,
ready the Fawn stumbles to offer herself up
d the Wolf-Cub weeps to be chosen.

e huddle-shawled lightning-faced warrior
mps his shaggy-trousered dance
an altar of blood.

Do not Pick up the Telephone

That plastic Buddha jars out a Karate screech

Before the soft words with their spores
The cosmetic breath of the gravestone

Death invented the phone it looks like the altar of death
Do not worship the telephone
It drags its worshippers into actual graves
With a variety of devices, through a variety of disguised voices

Sit godless when you hear the religious wail of the telephone

Do not think your house is a hide-out it is a telephone
Do not think you walk your own road, you walk down a telepho
Do not think you sleep in the hand of God you sleep in the
                                        mouthpiece of a telephc
Do not think your future is yours it waits upon a telephone
Do not think your thoughts are your own thoughts they are the
                                        toys of the telephc
Do not think these days are days they are the sacrificial priests of
                                        the telephc

The secret police of the telephone

O phone get out of my house
You are a bad god
Go and whisper on some other pillow
Do not lift your snake head in my house
Do not bite any more beautiful people

You plastic crab
Why is your oracle always the same in the end?
What rake off for you from the cemeteries?

Your silences are as bad
When you are needed, dumb with the malice of the clairvoyant

insane

The stars whisper together in your breathing
World's emptiness oceans in your mouthpiece
Stupidly your string dangles into the abysses
Plastic you are then stone a broken box of letters
And you cannot utter
Lies or truth, only the evil one
Makes you tremble with sudden appetite to see somebody undone

Blackening electrical connections
To where death bleaches its crystals
You swell and you writhe
You open your Buddha gape
You screech at the root of the house

Do not pick up the detonator of the telephone
A flame from the last day will come lashing out of the telephone
A dead body will fall out of the telephone

Do not pick up the telephone

From Gaudete

Collision with the earth has finally come—
How far can I fall?

A kelp, adrift
In my feeding substance

A mountain
Rooted in stone of heaven

A sea
Full of moon-ghost, with mangling waters

Dust on my head
Helpless to fit the pieces of water
A needle of many Norths

Ark of blood
Which is the magic baggage old men open
And find useless, at the great moment of need

Error on error
Perfumed
With a ribbon of fury

Once I said lightly
Even if the worst happens
We can't fall off the earth.

And again I said
No matter what fire cooks us
We shall be still in the pan together.

nd words twice as stupid.
ruly hell heard me.

e fell into the earth
nd I was devoured.

his is the maneater's skull.
hese brows were the Arc de Triomphe
o the gullet.

he deaf adder of appetite
oiled under. It spied through these nacelles
norant of death.

nd the whole assemblage flowed hungering through the
long ways.
 cry
uieted the valleys.

was looking for me.

vas looking for you.

ou were looking for me.

see the oak's bride in the oak's grasp.

uptials among prehistoric insects
he tremulous convulsion
he inching hydra strength
mong frilled lizards

157

Dropping twigs, and acorns, and leaves.
The oak is in bliss
Its roots
Lift arms that are a supplication
Crippled with stigmata
Like the sea-carved cliffs earth lifts
Loaded with dumb, uttering effigies
The oak seems to die and to be dead
In its love-act.

As I lie under it

In a brown leaf nostalgia

An acorn stupor.

A primrose petal's edge
Cuts the vision like laser.

And the eye of a hare
Strips the interrogator naked
Of all but some skin of terror—
A starry frost.

Who is this?
She reveals herself, and is veiled.
Somebody

Something grips by the nape
And bangs the brow, as against a wall
Against the untouchable veils

Of the hole which is bottomless

Till blood drips from the mouth.

Waving goodbye, from your banked hospital bed,
Waving, weeping, smiling, flushed
It happened
You knocked the world off, like a flower-vase.

It was the third time. And it smashed.

I turned
I bowed
In the morgue I kissed
Your temple's refrigerated glazed
As rained-on graveyard marble, my
Lips queasy, heart non-existent

And straightened
Into sun-darkness

Like a pillar over Athens

Defunct

In the blinding metropolis of cameras.

The swallow—rebuilding—
Collects the lot
From the sow's wallow.

But what I did only shifted the dust about.
And what crossed my mind
Crossed into outer space.

And for all rumours of me read obituary
What there truly remains of me
Is that very thing—my absence.

So how will you gather me?

I saw my keeper
Sitting in the sun—

If you can catch that, you are the falcon of falcons.

The grass-blade is not without
The loyalty that never was beheld.

And the blackbird
Sleeking from common anything and worm-dirt
Balances a precarious banner
Gold on black, terror and exultation.

The grim badger with armorial mask
Biting spade-steel, teeth and jaw-strake shattered,
Draws that final shuddering battle cry
Out of its backbone.

Me too,
Let me be one of your warriors.

Let your home
Be my home. Your people
My people.

I know well
You are not infallible

I know how your huge your unmanageable
Mass of bronze hair shrank to a twist
As thin as a silk scarf, on your skull,
And how your pony's eye darkened larger

Holding too lucidly the deep glimpse
After the humane killer

And I had to lift your hand for you

While your chin sank to your chest
With the sheer weariness
Of taking away from everybody
Your envied beauty, your much-desired beauty

Your hardly-used beauty

Of lifting away yourself
From yourself

And weeping with the ache of the effort

Sometimes it comes, a gloomy flap of lightning,
Like the flushed gossip
With the tale that kills

Sometimes it strengthens very slowly
What is already here—
A tree darkening the house.

The saviour
From these veils of wrinkle and shawls of ache

Like the sun
Which is itself cloudless and leafless

Was always here, is always as she was.

Calves harshly parted from their mamas
Stumble through all the hedges in the country
Hither thither crying day and night
Till their throats will only grunt and whistle.

After some days, a stupor sadness
Collects them again in their field.
They will never stray any more.
From now on, they only want each other.

So much for calves.
As for the tiger
He lies still
Like left luggage.

He is roaming the earth light, unseen.

He is safe.

Heaven and hell have both adopted him.

A bang—a burning—
I opened my eyes
In a vale crumbling with echoes.

A solitary dove
Cries in the tree—I cannot bear it.

From this centre
It wearies the compass.

Am I killed?
Or am I searching?

Is this the rainbow silking my body?

Which wings are these?

At the bottom of the Arctic sea, they say.

Or "Terrible as an army with banners."

If I wait, I am a castle
Built with blocks of pain.

If I set out
A kayak stitched with pain

❖

Your tree—your oak
A glare

Of black upward lightning, a wriggling grab
Momentary
Under the crumbling of stars.

A guard, a dancer
At the pure well of leaf.

Agony in the garden. Annunciation
Of clay, water and the sunlight.
They thunder under its roof.
Its agony is its temple.

Waist-deep, the black oak is dancing
And my eyes pause
On the centuries of its instant
As gnats
Try to winter in its wrinkles.

> The seas are thirsting
> Towards the oak.
>
> The oak is flying
> Astride the earth.

An October Salmon

He's lying in poor water, a yard or so depth of poor safety,
Maybe only two feet under the no-protection of an outleaning
                                                    small oak,
Half under a tangle of brambles.

After his two thousand miles, he rests,
Breathing in that lap of easy current
In his graveyard pool.

About six pounds weight,
Four years old at most, and a bare winter at sea—
But already a veteran,
Already a death-patched hero. So quickly it's over!

So briefly he roamed the gallery of marvels!
Such sweet months, so richly embroidered into earth's beauty-
                                                    dress,
Her life-robe—
Now worn out with her tirelessness, her insatiable quest,
Hangs in the flow, a frayed scarf—

An autumnal pod of his flower,
The mere hull of his prime, shrunk at shoulder and flank,

With the sea-going Aurora Borealis of his April power—
The primrose and violet of that first upfling in the estuary—
Ripened to muddy dregs,
The river reclaiming his sea-metals.

In the October light
He hangs there, patched with leper-cloths.

Death has already dressed him
In her clownish regimentals, her badges and decorations,
Mapping the completion of his service,
His face a ghoul-mask, a dinosaur of senility, and his whole body
A fungoid anemone of canker—

Can the caress of water ease him?
The flow will not let up for a minute.

What a change! From that covenant of Polar Light
To this shroud in a gutter!
What a death-in-life—to be his own spectre!
His living body become death's puppet!
Dolled by death in her crude paints and drapes
He haunts his own staring vigil
And suffers the subjection, and the dumbness,
And the humiliation of the role!

And that is how it is,
That is what is going on there, under the scrubby oak tree, hour
                                                 after hour,
That is what the splendour of the sea has come down to,
And the eye of ravenous joy—king of infinite liberty
In the flashing expanse, the bloom of sea-life,

On the surge-ride of energy, weightless,
Body simply the armature of energy
In that earliest sea-freedom, the savage amazement of life,
The salt mouthful of actual existence
With strength like light—

Yet this was always with him. This was inscribed in his egg.
This chamber of horrors is also home.
He was probably hatched in this very pool.

And this was the only mother he ever had, this uneasy channel of
                                                    minnows
Under the mill-wall, with bicycle wheels, car-tyres, bottles
And sunk sheets of corrugated iron.
People walking their dogs trail their evening shadows across him.
If boys see him they will try to kill him.

All this, too, is stitched into the torn richness,
The epic poise
That holds him so steady in his wounds, so loyal to his doom, so
                                                    patient
In the machinery of heaven.

Wadsworth Moor

Where the mothers
Gallop their souls

Where the howlings of heaven
Pour down onto earth
Looking for bodies
Of birds, animals, people

A happiness starts up, secret and wild,
Like a lark-song just out of hearing
Hidden in the wind

A silent evil joy
Like a star-broken stone
Who knows nothing more can happen to it
In its cradle-grave.

Mount Zion

Blackness
Was a building blocking my birth moon.
Its wall—my first world-direction—
Mount Zion's gravestone slab.

Above the kitchen window, that uplifted mass
Was a deadfall—
Darkening the sun of every day
Right to the eleventh hour.

Marched in under, gripped by elders
Like a jibbing calf
I knew what was coming.
The convicting holy eyes, the convulsed Moses' mouthings.
They were terrified too.
A mesmerised commissariat,
They terrified me, but they terrified each other.
And Christ was only a writhen bleeding worm
Who had given up the ghost.

Women bleak as Sunday rose-gardens,
Or crumpling to puff pastry, and cobwebbed with deaths.
Men in their prison-yard, at attention,
Exercising their cowed, shaven souls.
Lips stretching saliva, eyes fixed like the eyes
Of cockerels hung by the legs—their Hosanna
A bottomless cry
Beating itself numb again against Wesley's foundation stone.

Alarm shouts at dusk!
A cricket had rigged up its music
In a crack of Mount Zion wall.
A cricket! The news awful, the shouts awful, at dusk—
Like the bear alarm, at dusk, among smoky tents—
What was a cricket? How big is a cricket?

Long after I'd been smothered in bed
I could hear them
Riving at the religious stonework
With screwdrivers and cold chisels.

Curlews Lift

Out of the maternal watery blue lines

Stripped of all but their cry
Some twists of near-inedible sinew

They slough off
The robes of bilberry blue
The cloud-stained bogland

They veer up and eddy away over
The stone horns

They trail a long, dangling, falling aim
Across water

Lancing their voices
Through the skin of this light

Drinking the nameless and naked
Through trembling bills

Curlews in April
Hang their harps over the misty valleys

A wobbling water-call
A wet-footed god of the horizons

New moons sink into the heather
And full golden moons

Bulge over spent walls.

Rock has not Learned

Valleys are not aware
Heather and bog-cotton fit themselves
Into their snugness, vision sealed

And faces of people that appear
Moist-eyed, confronting the whole work

With cries that wince out
Just as they shape and tear clear

The whispery husk bones of faces

Are ground into fineness of light
By a weight
And shadowy violence
Of blind skylines revolving dumbly

Ignorant in ignorant air

When Men Got to the Summit

Light words forsook them.
They filled with heavy silence.

Houses came to support them,
But the hard, foursquare scriptures fractured
And the cracks filled with soft rheumatism.

Streets bent to the task
Of holding it all up
Bracing themselves, taking the strain
Till their vertebrae slipped.

The hills went on gently
Shaking their sieve.

Nevertheless, for some giddy moments
A television
Blinked from the wolf's lookout.

For Billy Holt

The longships got this far. Then
Anchored in nose and chin.

Badlands where outcast and outlaw
Fortified the hill-knowle's long outlook.

A far, veiled gaze of quietly
Homicidal appraisal.

A poverty
That cut rock lumps for words.

Requisitioned rain, then more rain,
For walls and roof.

Enfolding arms of sour hills
For company.

Blood in the veins
For amusement.

A graveyard
For homeland.

West Laithe

It is all
Happening to the sun.

The fallen sun
Is in the hands of water.

There are gulleys gouged in cold hills
By the sufferings of water

And gulleys
Cut in the cold fire

By the worn-out water of women
And the lost rivers of men.

Widdop

Where there was nothing
Somebody put a frightened lake.

Where there was nothing
Stony shoulders
Broadened to support it.

A wind from between the stars
Swam down to sniff at the trembling.

Trees, holding hands, eyes closed,
Acted at world.

Some heath-grass crept close, in fear.

Nothing else
Except when a gull blows through

A rip in the fabric

Out of nothingness into nothingness

Football at Slack

Between plunging valleys, on a bareback of hill
Men in bunting colours
Bounced, and their blown ball bounced.

The blown ball jumped, and the merry-coloured men
Spouted like water to head it.
The ball blew away downwind—

The rubbery men bounced after it.
The ball jumped up and out and hung on the wind
Over a gulf of treetops.
Then they all shouted together, and the ball blew back.

Winds from fiery holes in heaven
Piled the hills darkening around them
To awe them. The glare light
Mixed its mad oils and threw glooms.
Then the rain lowered a steel press.

Hair plastered, they all just trod water
To puddle glitter. And their shouts bobbed up
Coming fine and thin, washed and happy

While the humped world sank foundering
And the valleys blued unthinkable
Under depth of Atlantic depression—

But the wingers leapt, they bicycled in air
And the goalie flew horizontal

And once again a golden holocaust
Lifted the cloud's edge, to watch them.

Dead Farms, Dead Leaves

Cling to the long
Branch of world.

Stars sway the tree
Whose roots
Tighten on an atom.

The birds, beautiful-eyed, with soft cries,
The cattle of heaven,
Visit

And vanish.

Emily Brontë

The wind on Crow Hill was her darling.
His fierce, high tale in her ear was her secret.
But his kiss was fatal.

Through her dark Paradise ran
The stream she loved too well
That bit her breast.

The shaggy sodden king of that kingdom
Followed through the wall
And lay on her love-sick bed.

The curlew trod in her womb.

The stone weighed under her heart.

Her death is a baby-cry on the moor.

Heptonstall Old Church

A great bird landed here.

Its song drew men out of rock,
Living men out of bog and heather.

Its song put a light in the valleys
And harness on the long moors.

Its song brought a crystal from space
And set it in men's heads.

Then the bird died.

Its giant bones
Blackened and became a mystery.

The crystal in men's heads
Blackened and fell to pieces.

The valleys went out.
The moorland broke loose.

Heptonstall Cemetery

Wind slams across the tops.
The spray cuts upward.

You claw your way
Over a giant beating wing.

And Thomas and Walter and Edith
Are living feathers

Esther and Sylvia
Living feathers

Where all the horizons lift wings
A family of dark swans

And go beating low through storm-silver
Toward the Atlantic.

Tractor

The tractor stands frozen—an agony
To think of. All night
Snow packed its open entrails. Now a head-pincering gale,
A spill of molten ice, smoking snow,
Pours into its steel.
At white heat of numbness it stands
In the aimed hosing of ground-level fieriness.

It defies flesh and won't start.
Hands are like wounds already
Inside armour gloves, and feet are unbelievable
As if the toe-nails were all just torn off.
I stare at it in hatred. Beyond it
The copse hisses—capitulates miserably
In the fleeing, failing light. Starlings,
A dirtier sleetier snow, blow smokily, unendingly, over
Towards plantations Eastward.
All the time the tractor is sinking
Through the degrees, deepening
Into its hell of ice.

The starting lever
Cracks its action, like a snapping knuckle.
The battery is alive—but like a lamb
Trying to nudge its solid-frozen mother—
While the seat claims my buttock-bones, bites
With the space-cold of earth, which it has joined
In one solid lump.

I squirt commercial sure-fire
Down the black throat—it just coughs.
It ridicules me—a trap of iron stupidity
I've stepped into. I drive the battery

As if I were hammering and hammering
The frozen arrangement to pieces with a hammer
And it jabbers laughing pain-crying mockingly
Into happy life.

And stands
Shuddering itself full of heat, seeming to enlarge slowly
Like a demon demonstrating
A more-than-usually-complete materialization—
Suddenly it jerks from its solidarity
With the concrete, and lurches towards a stanchion
Bursting with superhuman well-being and abandon
Shouting Where Where?

Worse iron is waiting. Power-lift kneels,
Levers awake imprisoned deadweight,
Shackle-pins bedded in cast-iron cow-shit.
The blind and vibrating condemned obedience
Of iron to the cruelty of iron,
Wheels screeched out of their night-locks—

Fingers
Among the tormented
Tonnage and burning of iron

Eyes
Weeping in the wind of chloroform

And the tractor, streaming with sweat,
Raging and trembling and rejoicing.

Roe-Deer

In the dawn-dirty light, in the biggest snow of the year
Two blue-dark deer stood in the road, alerted.

They had happened into my dimension
The moment I was arriving just there.

They planted their two or three years of secret deerhood
Clear on my snow-screen vision of the abnormal

And hesitated in the all-way disintegration
And stared at me. And so for some lasting seconds

I could think the deer were waiting for me
To remember the password and sign

That the curtain had blown aside for a moment
And there where the trees were no longer trees, nor the
   road a road

The deer had come for me.

Then they ducked through the hedge, and upright they
   rode their legs
Away downhill over a snow-lonely field

Towards tree dark—finally
Seeming to eddy and glide and fly away up

Into the boil of big flakes.
The snow took them and soon their nearby hoofprints as
   well

Revising its dawn inspiration
Back to the ordinary.

Birth of Rainbow

This morning blue vast clarity of March sky
But a blustery violence of air, and a soaked overnight
Newpainted look to the world. The wind coming
Off the snowed moor in the South, razorish,
Heavy-bladed and head-cutting, off snow-powdered ridges.
Flooded ruts shook. Hoof-puddles flashed. A daisy
Mud-plastered unmixed its head from the mud.
The black and white cow, on the highest crest of the round
    ridge,
Stood under the end of a rainbow.
Head down licking something, full in the painful wind
That the pouring haze of the rainbow ignored.
She was licking her gawky black calf
Collapsed wet-fresh from the womb, blinking his eyes
In the low morning dazzling washed sun.
Black, wet as a collie from a river, as she licked him,
Finding his smells, learning his particularity.
A flag of bloody tissue hung from her back-end
Spreading and shining, pink-fleshed and raw, it flapped and
    coiled
In the unsparing wind. She positioned herself, uneasy
As we approached, nervous small footwork
On the hoof-ploughed drowned sod of the ruined field.
She made uneasy low noises, and her calf too
With his staring whites, mooed the full clear calf-note
Pure as woodwind, and tried to get up,
Tried to get his cantilever front legs
In operation, lifted his shoulders, hoisted to his knees,
Then hoisted his back end and lurched forward
On his knees and crumpling ankles, sliding in the mud
And collapsing plastered. She went on licking him.
She started eating the banner of thin raw flesh that
Spinnakered from her rear. We left her to it.

Blobbed antiseptic on to the sodden blood-dangle
Of his muddy birth-cord, and left her
Inspecting the new smell. The whole South West
Was black as nightfall.
Trailing squall-smokes hung over the moor leaning
And whitening towards us, then the world blurred
And disappeared in forty-five degree hail
And a gate-jerking blast. We got to cover.
Left to God the calf and his mother.

Couples under Cover

The ewes are in the shed
Under clapping wings of corrugated iron
Where entering rays of snow cut horizontal
Fiery and radio-active, a star-dust.
The oaks outside, half-digested
By a writhing white fire-snow off the hill-field
Burning to frails of charcoal
Roar blind, and swing blindly, a hill-top
Helpless self-defence. Snow
Is erasing them, whitening blanks
Against a dirty whiteness. The new jolly lambs
Are pleased with their nursery. A few cavorts
Keep trying their hind-legs—up and a twist,
So they stagger back to balance, bewildered
By the life that's working at them. Heads, safer,
Home in on udders, under-groin hot flesh-tent,
Hide eyes in muggy snugness. The ewes can't settle,
Heads bony and ratty with anxiety,
Keyed to every wind-shift, light-footed
To leap clear when the hill-top
Starts to peel off, or those tortured tree-oceans
Come blundering through the old stonework.
They don't appreciate the comfort.
They'd as soon be in midfield suffering
The twenty mile snow-gale of unprotection,
Ice-balls anaesthetising their back-end blood-tatters,
Watching and worrying while a lamb grows stranger—
A rumpy-humped skinned-looking rabbit
Whose hunger no longer works.

                        One day
Of slightly unnatural natural comfort, and the lambs
Will toss out into the snow, imperishable
Like trawlers, bobbing in gangs, while the world
Welters unconscious into whiteness.

Ravens

As we came through the gate to look at the few new lambs
On the skyline of lawn smoothness,
A raven bundled itself into air from midfield
And slid away under hard glistenings, low and guilty.
Sheep nibbling, kneeling to nibble the reluctant nibbled
     grass.
Sheep staring, their jaws pausing to think, then chewing
     again,
Then pausing. Over there a new lamb
Just getting up, bumping its mother's nose
As she nibbles the sugar coating off it
While the tattered banners of her triumph swing and drip
     from her rear-end.
She sneezes again and again, till she's emptied.
She carries on investigating her new present and seeing how
     it works.
Over here is something else. But you are still interested
In that new one, and its new spark of voice,
And its tininess.
Now over here, where the raven was,
Is what interests you next. Born dead,
Twisted like a scarf, a lamb of an hour or two,
Its insides, the various jellies and crimsons and
     transparencies
And threads and tissues pulled out
In straight lines, like tent ropes
From its upward belly opened like a lamb-wool slipper,
The fine anatomy of silvery ribs on display and the cavity,
The head also emptied through the eye-sockets,
The woolly limbs swathed in birth-yolk and impossible
To tell now which in all this field of quietly nibbling sheep
Was its mother. I explain

That it died being born. We should have been here, to
    help it.
So it died being born. "And did it cry?" you cry.
I pick up the dangling greasy weight by the hooves soft as
    dogs' pads
That had trodden only womb-water
And its raven-drawn strings dangle and trail,
Its loose head joggles, and "Did it cry?" you cry again.
Its two-fingered feet splay in their skin between the
    pressures
Of my finger and thumb. And there is another,
Just born, all black, splaying its tripod, inching its new
    points
Towards its mother, and testing the note
It finds in its mouth. But you have eyes now
Only for the tattered bundle of throwaway lamb.
"Did it cry?" you keep asking, in a three-year-old
    field-wide
Piercing persistence. "Oh yes" I say "it cried."

Though this one was lucky insofar
As it made the attempt into a warm wind
And its first day of death was blue and warm
The magpies gone quiet with domestic happiness
And skylarks not worrying about anything
And the blackthorn budding confidently
And the skyline of hills, after millions of hard years,
Sitting soft.

February 17th

A lamb could not get born. Ice wind
Out of a downpour dishclout sunrise. The mother
Lay on the mudded slope. Harried, she got up
And the blackish lump bobbed at her back-end
Under her tail. After some hard galloping,
Some manoeuvring, much flapping of the backward
Lump head of the lamb looking out,
I caught her with a rope. Laid her, head uphill
And examined the lamb. A blood-ball swollen
Tight in its black felt, its mouth gap
Squashed crooked, tongue stuck out, black-purple,
Strangled by its mother. I felt inside,
Past the noose of mother-flesh, into the slippery
Muscled tunnel, fingering for a hoof,
Right back to the port-hole of the pelvis.
But there was no hoof. He had stuck his head out too
    early
And his feet could not follow. He should have
Felt his way, tip-toe, his toes
Tucked up under his nose
For a safe landing. So I kneeled wrestling
With her groans. No hand could squeeze past
The lamb's neck into her interior
To hook a knee. I roped that baby head
And hauled till she cried out and tried
To get up and I saw it was useless. I went
Two miles for the injection and a razor.
Sliced the lamb's throat-strings, levered with a knife
Between the vertebrae and brought the head off
To stare at its mother, its pipes sitting in the mud
With all earth for a body. Then pushed
The neck-stump right back in, and as I pushed
She pushed. She pushed crying and I pushed gasping.

And the strength
Of the birth push and the push of my thumb
Against that wobbly vertebra were deadlock,
A to-fro futility. Till I forced
A hand past and got a knee. Then like
Pulling myself to the ceiling with one finger
Hooked in a loop, timing my effort
To her birth push groans, I pulled against
The corpse that would not come. Till it came.
And after it the long, sudden, yolk-yellow
Parcel of life
In a smoking slither of oils and soups and syrups—
And the body lay born, beside the hacked-off head.

Sheep

I

The sheep has stopped crying.
All morning in her wire-mesh compound
On the lawn, she has been crying
For her vanished lamb. Yesterday they came.
Then her lamb could stand, in a fashion,
And make some tiptoe cringing steps.
Now he has disappeared.
He was only half the proper size.
And his cry was wrong. It was not
A dry little hard bleat, a baby-cry
Over a flat tongue, it was human,
It was a despairing human smooth Oh!
Like no lamb I ever heard. Its hindlegs
Cowered in under its lumped spine,
Its feeble hips leaned towards
Its shoulders for support. Its stubby
White wool pyramid head, on a tottery neck,
Had sad and defeated eyes, pinched, pathetic,
Too small, and it cried all the time
Oh! Oh! staggering towards
Its alert, baffled, stamping, storming mother
Who feared our intentions. He was too weak
To find her teats, or to nuzzle up in under,
He hadn't the gumption. He was fully
Occupied just standing, then shuffling
Towards where she'd removed to. She knew
He wasn't right, she couldn't
Make him out. Then his rough-curl legs,
So stoutly built, and hooved
With real quality tips,

Just got in the way, like a loose bundle
Of firewood he was cursed to manage,
Too heavy for him, lending sometimes
Some support, but no strength, no real help.
When we sat his mother on her tail, he mouthed her teat,
Slobbered a little, but after a minute
Lost aim and interest, his muzzle wandered,
He was managing a difficulty
Much more urgent and important. By evening
He could not stand. It was not
That he could not thrive, he was born
With everything but the will—
That can be deformed, just like a limb.
Death was more interesting to him.
Life could not get his attention.
So he died, with the yellow birth-mucus
Still in his cardigan.
He did not survive a warm summer night.
Now his mother has started crying again.
The wind is oceanic in the elms
And the blossom is all set.

II

The mothers have come back
From the shearing, and behind the hedge
The woe of sheep is like a battlefield
In the evening, when the fighting is over,
And the cold begins, and the dew falls,
And bowed women move with water.
Mother Mother Mother the lambs
Are crying, and the mothers are crying.
Nothing can resist that probe, that cry
Of a lamb for its mother, or a ewe's crying

For its lamb. The lambs cannot find
Their mothers among those shorn strangers.
A half-hour they have lamented,
Shaking their voices in desperation.
Bald brutal-voiced mothers braying out,
Flat-tongued lambs chopping off hopelessness
Their hearts are in panic, their bodies
Are a mess of woe, woe they cry,
They mingle their trouble, a music
Of worse and worse distress, a worse entangling,
They hurry out little notes
With all their strength, cries searching this way and that.
The mothers force out sudden despair, blaaa!
On restless feet, with wild heads.

Their anguish goes on and on, in the June heat.
Only slowly their hurt dies, cry by cry,
As they fit themselves to what has happened.

Coming Down Through Somerset

I flash-glimpsed in the headlights—the high moment
Of driving through England—a killed badger
Sprawled with helpless legs. Yet again
Manoeuvred lane-ends, retracked, waited
Out of decency for headlights to die,
Lifted by one warm hindleg in the world-night
A slain badger. August dust-heat. Beautiful,
Beautiful, warm, secret beast. Bedded him
Passenger, bleeding from the nose. Brought him close
Into my life. Now he lies on the beam
Torn from a great building. Beam waiting two years
To be built into new building. Summer coat
Not worth skinning off him. His skeleton—for the future.
Fangs, handsome concealed. Flies, drumming,
Bejewel his transit. Heatwave ushers him hourly
Towards his underworlds. A grim day of flies
And sunbathing. Get rid of that badger.
A night of shrunk rivers, glowing pastures,
Sea-trout shouldering up through trickles. Then the sun
    again.
Waking like a torn-out eye. How strangely
He stays on into the dawn—how quiet
The dark bear-claws, the long frost-tipped guard hairs!
Get rid of that badger today.
And already the flies.
More passionate, bringing their friends. I don't want
To bury and waste him. Or skin him (it is too late).
Or hack off his head and boil it
To liberate his masterpiece skull. I want him
To stay as he is. Sooty gloss-throated,
With his perfect face. Paws so tired,
Power-body relegated. I want him
To stop time. His strength staying, bulky,

Blocking time. His rankness, his bristling wildness,
His thrillingly painted face.
A badger on my moment of life.
Not years ago, like the others, but now.
I stand
Watching his stillness, like an iron nail
Driven, flush to the head,
Into a yew post. Something
Has to stay.

Now You have to Push

Your hands
Lumpish roots of earth cunning
So wrinkle-scarred, such tomes
Of what has been collecting centuries
At the bottom of so many lanes
Where roofs huddle smoking, and cattle
Trample the ripeness

Now you have to push your face
So tool-worn, so land-weathered,
This patch of ancient, familiar locale,
Your careful little moustache,
Your gangly long broad Masai figure
Which you decked so dapperly to dances,
Your hawser and lever strength
Which you used, so recklessly,
Like a tractor, guaranteed unbreakable

Now you have to push it all—
Just as you loved to push the piled live hedge-boughs—
Into a gathering blaze

And as you loved to linger late into the twilight,
Coaxing the last knuckle embers,
Now you have to stay
Right on, into total darkness

The Formal Auctioneer

Is trying to sell cattle. He is like a man
Walking noisily through a copse
Where nothing will be flushed. All eyes watch.
The weathered, rooty, bushy pile of faces,
A snaggle of faces
Like pulled-out and heaped-up old moots,
The natural root archives
Of mid-Devon's mud-lane annals,
Watch and hide inside themselves
Absorbing the figures like weather,
Or if they bid, bid invisibly, visit
The bidding like night-foxes,
Slink in and out of bidding
As if they were no such fools
To be caught interested in anything,
Escaping a bidding with the secret
Celebration of a bargain, a straight gain
And that much now in hand.

When you were among them
Hidden in your own bidding, you stood tall,
A tree with two knot-eyes, immovable,
A root among roots, without leaf,
Buying a bullock, with the eye-gesture
Of a poker-player
Dead-panning his hand. Deep-root weathering
The heat-wave of a bargain.

From PROMETHEUS ON HIS CRAG

9

Now I know I never shall

Be let stir.
The man I fashioned and the god I fashioned
Dare not let me stir.

This leakage of cry these face-ripples
Calculated for me—for mountain water
Dammed to powerless stillness.

What secret stays
Stilled under my stillness?
Not even I know.

Only he knows—that bird, that
Filthy-gleeful emissary and
The hieroglyph he makes of my entrails

Is all he tells.

10

Prometheus on his crag
Began to admire the vulture
It knew what it was doing

It went on doing it
Swallowing not only his liver
But managing also to digest its guilt

And hang itself again just under the sun
Like a heavenly weighing scales
Balancing the gift of life

And the cost of the gift
Without a tremor
As if both were nothing.

20

Prometheus on his crag

Pondered the vulture. Was this bird
His unborn half-self, some hyena
Afterbirth, some lump of his mother?

Or was it his condemned human ballast—
His dying and his death, torn daily
From his immortality?

Or his blowtorch godhead
Puncturing those horrendous holes
In his human limits?

Was it his prophetic familiar?
The Knowledge, pebble-eyed,
Of the fates to be suffered in his image?

Was it the flapping, tattered hole—
The nothing door
Of his entry, draughting through him?

Or was it atomic law—
Was Life his transgression?
Was he the punished criminal aberration?

Was it the fire he had stolen?
Nowhere to go and now his pet,
And only him to feed on?

Or the supernatural spirit itself
That he had stolen from,
Now stealing from him the natural flesh?

Or was it the earth's enlightenment—
Was he an uninitiated infant
Mutilated towards alignment?

Or was it his anti-self—
The him-shaped vacuum
In unbeing, pulling to empty him?

Or was it, after all, the Helper
Coming again to pick at the crucial knot
Of all his bonds . . .?

Image after image. Image after image. As the vulture
Circled

Circled.

From ADAM AND THE SACRED NINE

And the Falcon Came

The gunmetal feathers
Of would not be put aside, would not falter.

The wing-knuckles
Of dividing the mountain, of hurling the world away behind him.

With the bullet-brow
Of burying himself head-first and ahead
Of his delicate bones, into the target
Collision.

The talons
Of a first, last, single blow
Of grasping complete the crux of rays.

With the tooled bill
Of plucking out the ghost
And feeding it to his eye-flame

Of stripping down the loose, hot flutter of earth
To its component parts
For the reconstitution of Falcon

With the eye
Of explosion of Falcon.

The Wild Duck

                         got up with a cry
Shook off her Arctic swaddling

Pitched from the tower of the North Wind
And came spanking across water

The wild duck, fracturing egg-zero,
Left her mother the snow in her shawl of stars
Abandoned her father the black wind in his beard of stars

Got up out of the ooze before dawn

Now hangs her whispering arrival
Between earth-glitter and heaven-glitter

Calling softly to the fixed lakes

As earth gets up in the frosty dark, at the back of the Pole Star
And flies into dew
Through the precarious crack of light

Quacking Wake Wake

The Swift Comes the Swift

Casts aside the two-arm two-leg article—
The pain instrument
Flesh and soft entrails and nerves, and is off.

Hurls itself as if again beyond where it fell among roofs
Out through the lightning-split in the great oak of light

One wing below mineral limit
One wing above dream and number

Shears between life and death

Whiskery snarl-gape already gone ahead
The eyes in possession ahead

Screams guess its trajectory
Meteorite puncturing the veils of worlds

Whipcrack, the ear's glimpse
Is the smudge it leaves

Hunting the winged mote of death into the sun's retina
Picking the nymph of life
Off the mirror of the lake of atoms

Till the Swift
Who falls out of the blindness, swims up
From the molten, rejoins itself

Shadow to shadow—resumes proof, nests
Papery ashes
Of the uncontainable burning.

And Owl

Floats. A masked soul listening for death.
Death listening for a soul.
Small mouths and their incriminations are suspended.
Only the centre moves.

Constellations stand in awe. And the trees very still, the fields very
    still
As the Owl becalms deeper
To stillness.
Two eyes, fixed in the heart of heaven.

Nothing is neglected, in the Owl's stare.
The womb opens and the cry comes
And the shadow of the creature
Circumscribes its fate. And the Owl

Screams, again ripping the bandages off
Because of the shape of its throat, as if it were a torture
Because of the shape of its face, as if it were a prison
Because of the shape of its talons, as if they were inescapable

Heaven screams. Earth screams. Heaven eats. Earth is eaten.

And earth eats and heaven is eaten.

The Dove Came

Her breast big with rainbows
She was knocked down

The dove came, her wings clapped lightning
That scattered like twigs
She was knocked down

The dove came, her voice of thunder
A piling heaven of silver and violet
She was knocked down

She gave the flesh of her breast, and they ate her
She gave the milk of her blood, they drank her

The dove came again, a sun-blinding

And ear could no longer hear

Mouth was a disembowelled bird
Where the tongue tried to stir like a heart

And the dove alit
In the body of thorns.

Now deep in the dense body of thorns
A soft thunder
Nests her rainbows

And the Phoenix has Come

Its voice
Is the blade of the desert, a fighting of light
Its voice dangles glittering
In the soft valley of dew

Its voice flies flaming and dripping flame
Slowly across the dusty sky
Its voice burns in a rich heap
Of mountains that seem to melt

Its feathers shake from the eye
Its ashes smoke from the breath

Flesh trembles
The altar of its death and its birth

Where it descends
Where it offers itself up

And naked the newborn
Crows in the blaze

The Song

Did not want the air
Or the distant sky

The song
Did not want the hill-slope from which it echoed

Did not want the leaves
Through which its vibrations ran

Did not want the stones whose indifference
It nevertheless ruffled

Did not want the water

The song did not want its own mouth
Was careless of its own throat
Of the lungs and veins
From which it poured

The song made of joy
Searched, even like a lament

For what did not exist

Pouring out over the empty grave
Of what was not yet born

From EARTH-NUMB

Earth-Numb

Dawn—a smouldering fume of dry frost.
Sky-edge of red-hot iron.
Daffodils motionless—some fizzled out.
The birds—earth-brim simmering.
Sycamore buds unsticking—the leaf out-crumpling, purplish.

The pheasant cock's glare-cry. Jupiter ruffling softly.

Hunting salmon. And hunted
And haunted by apparitions from tombs
Under the smoothing tons of dead element
In the river's black canyons.

The lure is a prayer. And my searching—
Like the slow sun.
A prayer, like a flower opening.
A surgeon operating
On an open heart, with needles—

And bang! the river grabs at me

A mouth-flash, an electrocuting malice
Like a trap, trying to rip life off me—
And the river stiffens alive,
The black hole thumps, the whole river hauls
And I have one.

A piling voltage hums, jamming me stiff—
Something terrified and terrifying
Gleam-surges to and fro through me
From the river to the sky, from the sky into the river

Uprooting dark bedrock, shatters it in air,
Cartwheels across me, slices thudding through me
As if I were the current—

Till the fright flows all one way down the line

And a ghost grows solid, a hoverer,
A lizard green slither, banner heavy—

Then the wagging stone pebble head
Trying to think on shallows—

Then the steel spectre of purples
From the forge of water
Gagging on emptiness

As the eyes of incredulity
Fix their death-exposure of the celandine and the cloud.

A Motorbike

We had a motorbike all through the war
In an outhouse—thunder, flight, disruption
Cramped in rust, under washing, abashed, outclassed
By the Brens, the Bombs, the Bazookas elsewhere.

The war ended, the explosions stopped.
The men surrendered their weapons
And hung around limply.
Peace took them all prisoner.
They were herded into their home towns.
A horrible privation began
Of working a life up out of the avenues
And the holiday resorts and the dance-halls.

Then the morning bus was as bad as any labour truck,
The foreman, the boss, as bad as the S.S.
And the ends of the street and the bends of the road
And the shallowness of the shops and the shallowness of the beer
And the sameness of the next town
Were as bad as electrified barbed wire.
The shrunk-back war ached in their testicles
And England dwindled to the size of a dog-track.

So there came this quiet young man
And he bought our motorbike for twelve pounds.
And he got it going, with difficulty.
He kicked it into life—it erupted
Out of the six year sleep, and he was delighted.

A week later, astride it, before dawn,
A misty frosty morning,
He escaped

Into a telegraph pole
On the long straight west of Swinton.

Deaf School

The deaf children were monkey-nimble, fish-tremulous and
                                                    sudden.
Their faces were alert and simple
Like faces of little animals, small night lemurs caught in the flash-
                                                    light.
They lacked a dimension,
They lacked a subtle wavering aura of sound and responses to
                                                    sound.
The whole body was removed
From the vibration of air, they lived through the eyes,
The clear simple look, the instant full attention.
Their selves were not woven into a voice
Which was woven into a face
Hearing itself, its own public and audience,
An apparition in camouflage, an assertion in doubt—
Their selves were hidden, and their faces looked out of hiding.
What they spoke with was a machine,
A manipulation of fingers, a control-panel of gestures
Out there in the alien space
Separated from them—

Their unused faces were simple lenses of watchfulness
Simple pools of earnest watchfulness

Their bodies were like their hands
Nimbler than bodies, like the hammers of a piano,
A puppet agility, a simple mechanical action
A blankness of hieroglyph
A stylized lettering
Spelling out approximate signals

While the self looked through, out of the face of simple
concealment
A face not merely deaf, a face in darkness, a face unaware,
A face that was simply the front skin of the self concealed and
separate

Life is Trying to be Life

Death also is trying to be life.
Death is in the sperm like the ancient mariner
With his horrible tale.

Death mews in the blankets—is it a kitten?
It plays with dolls but cannot get interested.
It stares at the windowlight and cannot make it out.
It wears baby clothes and is patient.
It learns to talk, watching the others' mouths.
It laughs and shouts and listens to itself numbly.
It stares at people's faces
And sees their skin like a strange moon, and stares at the grass
In its position just as yesterday.
And stares at its fingers and hears: "Look at that child!"
Death is a changeling
Tortured by daisy chains and Sunday bells
It is dragged about like a broken doll
By little girls playing at mothers and funerals.
Death only wants to be life. It cannot quite manage.

Weeping it is weeping to be life
As for a mother it cannot remember.

Death and Death and Death, it whispers
With eyes closed, trying to feel life

Like the shout in joy
Like the glare in lightning
That empties the lonely oak.
                              And that is the death
In the antlers of the Irish Elk. It is the death

In the cave-wife's needle of bone. Yet it still is not death—

Or in the shark's fang which is a monument
Of its lament
On a headland of life.

Speech out of Shadow

Not your eyes, but what they disguise

Not your skin, with just that texture and light
But what uses it as cosmetic

Not your nose——to be or not to be beautiful
But what it is the spy for

Not your mouth, not your lips, not their adjustments
But the maker of the digestive tract

Not your breasts
Because they are diversion and deferment

Not your sexual parts, your proffered rewards
Which are in the nature of a flower
Technically treacherous

Not the webs of your voice, your poise, your tempo
Your drug of a million micro-signals

But the purpose.

The unearthly stone in the sun.

The glare
Of the falcon, behind its hood

Tamed now
To its own mystifications

And the fingerings of men.

Night Arrival of Sea-Trout

Honeysuckle hanging her fangs.
Foxglove rearing her open belly.
Dogrose touching the membrane.

Through the dew's mist, the oak's mass
Comes plunging, tossing dark antlers.

Then a shattering
Of the river's hole, where something leaps out—

An upside-down, buried heaven
Snarls, moon-mouthed, and shivers.

Summer dripping stars, biting at the nape.
Lobworms coupling in saliva.
Earth singing under her breath.

And out in the hard corn a horned god
Running and leaping
With a bat in his drum.

From Seven Dungeon Songs

I

Dead, she became space-earth
Broken to pieces.
Plants nursed her death, unearthed her goodness.

But her murderer, mad-innocent
Sucked at her offspring, reckless of blood,
Consecrating them in fire, muttering
It is good to be God.

He used familiar hands
Incriminating many,
And he borrowed mouths, leaving names
Being himself nothing

But a tiger's sigh, a wolf's music
A song on a lonely road

What it is
Risen out of mud, fallen from space
That stares through a face.

II

Face was necessary—I found face.
Hands—I found hands.

I found shoulders, I found legs
I found all bits and pieces.

We were me, and lay quiet.
I got us all of a piece, and we lay quiet.

221

We just lay.
Sunlight had prepared a wide place

And we lay there.
Air nursed us.

We recuperated.
While maggots blackened to seeds, and blood warmed its stone.

Only still something
Stared at me and screamed

Stood over me, black across the sun,
And mourned me, and would not help me get up.

III

The earth locked out the light,
Blocking the light, like a door locked.
But a crack of light

Between sky and earth, was enough.
He called it, Earth's halo.

And the lizard spread of his fingers
Reached for it.

He called it, The leakage of air
Into this suffocation of earth.

And the gills of his rib-cage
Gulped to get more of it.

His lips pressed to its coolness
Like an eye to a crack.

He lay like the already-dead

Tasting the tears
Of the wind-shaken and weeping
Tree of light.

IV

I walk
Unwind with activity of legs
The tangled ball
Which was once the orderly circuit of my body

Some night in the womb
All my veins and capillaries were taken out
By some evil will
And knotted in a great ball and stuffed back inside me

Now I rush to and fro
I try to attach a raw broken end
To some steady place, then back away
I look for people with clever fingers
Who might undo me

The horrible ball just comes
People's fingers snarl it worse

I hurl myself
To jerk out the knot
Or snap it

And come up short

So dangle and dance
The dance of unbeing

V

If mouth could open its cliff
If ear could unfold from this strata
If eyes could split their rock and peep out finally

If hands of mountain-fold
Could get a proper purchase
If feet of fossil could lift

If head of lakewater and weather
If body of horizon
If whole body and balancing head

If skin of grass could take messages
And do its job properly

If spine of earth-foetus
Could unfurl

If man-shadow out there moved to my moves

The speech that works air
Might speak me

TV Off

He hears lithe trees and last leaves swatting the glass—

Staring into flames, through the grille of age
Like a late fish, face clothed with fungus,
Keeping its mouth upstream.

Remorseful for what nobody any longer suffers
Nostalgic for what he would not give twopence to see back
Hopeful for what he will not miss when it fails

Who lay a night and a day and a night and a day
Golden-haired, while his friend beside him
Attending a small hole in his brow
Ripened black.

Prospero and Sycorax

She knows, like Ophelia,
The task has swallowed him.
She knows, like George's dragon,
Her screams have closed his helmet.

She knows, like Jocasta,
It is over.
He prefers
Blindness.

She knows, like Cordelia,
He is not himself now,
And what speaks through him must be discounted—
Though it will be the end of them both.

She knows, like God,
He has found
Something
Easier to live with—

His death, her death.

Tiger-Psalm

The tiger kills hungry. The machine-guns
Talk, talk, talk across their Acropolis.
The tiger
Kills expertly, with anaesthetic hand.
The machine-guns
Carry on arguing in heaven
Where numbers have no ears, where there is no blood.
The tiger
Kills frugally, after close inspection of the map.
The machine-guns shake their heads,
They go on chattering statistics.
The tiger kills by thunderbolt:
God of his own salvation.
The machine-guns
Proclaim the Absolute, according to morse,
In a code of bangs and holes that makes men frown.
The tiger
Kills with beautiful colours in his face,
Like a flower painted on a banner.
The machine-guns
Are not interested.
They laugh. They are not interested. They speak and
Their tongues burn soul-blue, haloed with ashes,
Puncturing the illusion.
The tiger
Kills and licks his victim all over carefully.
The machine-guns
Leave a crust of blood hanging on the nails
In an orchard of scrap-iron.
The tiger
Kills
With the strength of five tigers, kills exalted.
The machine-guns

Permit themselves a snigger. They eliminate the error
With a to-fro dialectic
And the point proved stop speaking.
The tiger
Kills like a fall of a cliff, one-sinewed with the earth,
Himalayas under eyelid, Ganges under fur—

Does not kill.

Does not kill. The tiger blesses with a fang.
The tiger does not kill but opens a path
Neither of Life nor of Death:
The tiger within the tiger:
The Tiger of the Earth.
                    O Tiger!
O Brother of the Viper!
                    O Beast in Blossom!

The Stone

Has not yet been cut.
It is too heavy already
For consideration. Its edges
Are so super-real, already,
And at this distance,
They cut real cuts in the unreal
Stuff of just thinking. So I leave it.
Somewhere it is.
Soon it will come.
I shall not carry it. With horrible life
It will transport its face, with sure strength,
To sit over mine, wherever I look,
Instead of hers.
It will even have across its brow
Her name.

Somewhere it is coming to the end
Of its million million years—
Which have worn her out.
It is coming to the beginning
Of her million million million years
Which will wear out it.

Because she will never move now
Till it is worn out.
She will not move now
Till everything is worn out.

The Woman in the Valley

Which ones
Of the eager faces, garlic or iris
Come back for the new herons?

Once the floods have wiped away their pollen
Have undressed them
And folded them into winter?

Venus and Jupiter, year in and year out,
Contend for the crown
Of morning star and of evening star.

And the fish worship the source, bowed and fervent,
But their hearts are water.

The river walks in the valley singing
Letting her veils blow

A novelty from the red side of Adam.

April in the lift of her arm
November in the turn of her shoulder

As if her sauntering were a long stillness.

She who has not once tasted death.

A God

Pain was pulled down over his eyes like a fool's hat.
They pressed electrodes of pain through the parietals.

He was helpless as a lamb
Which cannot be born
Whose head hangs under its mother's anus.

Pain was stabbed through his palm, at the crutch of the M,
Made of iron, from earth's core.
From that pain he hung,
As if he were being weighed.
The cleverness of his fingers availed him
As the bullock's hooves, in the offal bin,
Avail the severed head
Hanging from its galvanized hook.

Pain was hooked through his foot.
From that pain, too, he hung
As on display.
His patience had meaning only for him
Like the sanguine upside-down grin
Of a hanging half-pig.

There, hanging,
He accepted the pain beneath his ribs
Because he could no more escape it
Than the poulterer's hanging hare,
Hidden behind eyes growing concave,
Can escape
What has replaced its belly.

He could not understand what had happened.

Or what he had become.

Salmon Eggs

The salmon were just down there—
Shuddering together, caressing each other,
Emptying themselves for each other—

Now beneath flood-murmur
They curve away deathwards.
                                        January haze,
With a veined yolk of sun. In bone-damp cold
I lean and watch the water, listening to water
Till my eyes forget me

And the piled flow supplants me, the mud-blooms

All this ponderous light of everlasting
Collapsing away under its own weight

Mastodon ephemera

Mud-curdling, bull-dozing, hem-twinkling
Caesarean of heaven and earth, unfelt

With exhumations and delirious advents—

                                        Catkins
Wriggle at their mother's abundance. The spider clings to his craft.

Something else is going on in the river

More vital than death—death here seems a superficiality
Of small scaly limbs, parasitical. More grave than life
Whose reflex jaws and famished crystals
Seem incidental
To this telling—these toilings of plasm—

The melt of mouthing silence, the charge of light
Dumb with immensity.
                              The river goes on
Sliding through its place, undergoing itself
In its wheel.

                    I make out the sunk foundations
Of burst crypts, a bedrock
Time-hewn, time-riven altar. And this is the liturgy
Of the earth's tidings—harrowing, crowned—a travail
Of raptures and rendings.

                              Sanctus Sanctus
Swathes the blessed issue.

                              Perpetual mass
Of the waters
Wells from the cleft.

                    It is the raw vent
Of the nameless
Teeming inside atoms—and inside the haze
And inside the sun and inside the earth.

It is the font, brimming with touch and whisper,
Swaddling the egg.

                    Only birth matters
Say the river's whorls.

                    And the river
Silences everything in a leaf-mouldering hush
Where sun rolls bare, and earth rolls

And mind condenses on old haws.

That Morning

We came where the salmon were so many,
So steady, so spaced, so far-aimed
On their inner map, England could add

Only the sooty twilight of South Yorkshire
Hung with the drumming drift of Lancasters
Till the world had seemed capsizing slowly.

Solemn to stand there in the pollen light
Waist-deep in wild salmon swaying massed
As from the hand of God. There the body

Separated, golden and imperishable,
From its doubting thought—a spirit beacon
Lit by the power of the salmon

That came on, came on, and kept on coming
As if we flew slowly, their formations
Lifting us toward some dazzle of blessing

One wrong thought might darken. As if the fallen
World and salmon were over. As if these
Were the imperishable fish

That had let the world pass away—

There, in a mauve light of drifted lupins,
They hung in the cupped hands of mountains

Made of tingling atoms. It had happened.
Then for a sign that we were where we were
Two gold bears came down and swam like men

Beside us. And dived like children.
And stood in deep water as on a throne
Eating pierced salmon off their talons.

So we found the end of our journey.

So we stood, alive in the river of light
Among the creatures of light, creatures of light.

NOTE

The poems in the earlier part of this collection were intended to communicate in their own terms, without the reader needing to consult any note. But here and there in the later pages are poems prompted by particular circumstances of composition, as parts of longer sequences or a collaboration, where some other element of the whole carried the burden of exposition and context. The poems in question will be interpreted more easily, I imagine, if the reader has some hint of what that background is, in each case.

CROW   This is a sequence of poems relating the birth, upbringing and adventures of a protagonist of that name.

CAVE BIRDS   This is a sequence of twenty-nine poems written to accompany drawings—of imaginary birds—by Leonard Baskin. The poems plot the course of a symbolic drama, concerning disintegration and re-integration, with contrapuntal roles played by birds and humans. For the four poems printed here the drawings cannot be reproduced, so it might help to know that the Executioner (page 137) is a giant raven; the Knight (page 138) is a decomposing bird of the Crow type; Bride and Groom (page 140) are human beings with bird attributes, and the Risen (page 142) is a falcon, the full-fledged emergence of a Horus. Throughout the original sequence the interdependence between drawings and verses is quite close.

GAUDETE   This is a long story in verse which outlines the last day of a changeling—a creature substituted for an Anglican clergyman, as an all but perfect duplicate, by powers of the other world, while the real clergyman remains in the other world as their prisoner (like Thomas the Rhymer in the Scots ballad). At the destruction of the changeling, the man of flesh and blood reappears, and the poems here are taken from his notebook—his diary of coming to his senses, or of trying to come to his senses.

REMAINS OF ELMET   These poems come from a sequence written as texts to accompany photographs, by Fay Godwin, of the Calder Valley and environs in West Yorkshire, where I spent my early years, and where I have lived occasionally since. It is a landscape of Pennine moorland and the remains of the small towns that grew up with the wool, weaving, spinning and clothing.

PROMETHEUS ON HIS CRAG   These pieces come from a sequence, with this title, in my collection *Moortown*. They grew from the background material of the drama *Orghast*, which I made for Peter Brook's International Theatre Research Group and which was performed at Persepolis on the occasion of the 1970 Shiraz Festival. Our drama combined the *Prometheus Bound* of Aeschylus, Calderon's *Life is a Dream*—both of these stories had early roots in Persia—and archaic bits of myth, mainly early Persian, associated with the figure of Prometheus. It revolved around the complementary fates of this semi-divine figure nailed to the mountain summit and the disinherited figure chained in the mountain's heart.

MOORTOWN   The sequence entitled MOORTOWN in my collection of the same name, from which the pieces here are selected, is made up of passages taken from a verse farming diary that I kept for a while, the location being mid-Devon.

ADAM AND THE SACRED NINE   These poems form part of a small sequence in which Adam, fallen prostrate, is visited by nine birds who each in turn bring their gift of 'how to live', for him to accept or reject.

T.H.